D1459893

11 New Projects from Open Gate

Traditional
Fat Quarter Quilts

Monique Dillard

C&T PUBLISHING

Text copyright © 2012 by Monique Dillard

Photography and Artwork copyright © 2012 by C&T Publishing, Inc.

Publisher: Amy Marson

Creative Director: Gailen Runge

Acquisitions Editor: Susanne Woods

Editors: Lynn Koolish and Deb Rowden

Technical Editors: Carolyn Aune and Priscilla Read

Cover / Book Designer: Kristy Zacharias

Page Layout Artist / Production Coordinator: Zinnia Heinzmann

Production Editor: S. Michele Fry

Illustrator: Aliza Shalit

Photography by Christina Carty-Francis and Diane Pedersen of C&T Publishing, Inc., unless otherwise noted

Published by C&T Publishing, Inc., P.O. Box 1456, Lafayette, CA 94549

All rights reserved. No part of this work covered by the copyright hereon may be used in any form or reproduced by any means—graphic, electronic, or mechanical, including photocopying, recording, taping, or information storage and retrieval systems—without written permission from the publisher. The copyrights on individual artworks are retained by the artists as noted in *Traditional Fat Quarter Quilts*. These designs may be used to make items only for personal use or donation to non-profit groups for sale or for display only at events, provided the following credit is included on a conspicuous label: Designs copyright © 2012 by Monique Dillard from the book *Traditional Fat Quarter Quilts* from C&T Publishing, Inc. Permission for all other purposes must be requested in writing from C&T Publishing, Inc.

Attention Teachers: C&T Publishing, Inc., encourages you to use this book as a text for teaching. Contact us at 800-284-1114 or www.ctpub.com for lesson plans and information about the C&T Creative Troupe.

We take great care to ensure that the information included in our products is accurate and presented in good faith, but no warranty is provided nor are results guaranteed. Having no control over the choices of materials or procedures used, neither the author nor C&T Publishing, Inc., shall have any liability to any person or entity with respect to any loss or damage caused directly or indirectly by the information contained in this book. For your convenience, we post an up-to-date listing of corrections on our website (www.ctpub.com). If a correction is not already noted, please contact our customer service department at ctinfo@ctpub.com or at P.O. Box 1456, Lafayette, CA 94549.

Trademark (™) and registered trademark (®) names are used throughout this book. Rather than use the symbols with every occurrence of a trademark or registered trademark name, we are using the names only in the editorial fashion and to the benefit of the owner, with no intention of infringement.

Library of Congress Cataloging-in-Publication Data

Dillard, Monique, 1967-

  Traditional Fat Quarter Quilts : 11 New Projects from Open Gate / Monique Dillard.

    p. cm.

  ISBN 978-1-60705-437-5 (soft cover)

1. Quilting--Patterns. 2. Patchwork--Patterns. 3. Quilts--Patterns. I. Title.

  TT835.D5484 2011

  746.46--dc23

                          2011026885

Printed in China

10 9 8 7 6 5 4 3 2 1

Acknowledgments

When I am working on a new book, I rely heavily on my wonderful friends and family to help me complete the projects. I would like to thank them for all their help and support, as well as their love and encouragement.

Many thanks go to my wonderful and talented friends: Joyce Davis, Peggy Drake, Kathy Rosecrance, and Sue Glorch, who helped me piece the quilts in this book. Thanks to LeAnne Olson, Danette Gonzalez, and Sue Glorch, who provided the creative machine quilting, and to proofreaders Sue Glorch, Kathy Rosecrance, Katie Otto, and Noreen Ayotte.

Thanks go to Maywood Studio for supplying me with Olde World Style, my debut fabric line. Also, thanks to Moda for always providing me with their wonderful fabric. I would also like to thank C&T for publishing my books and for their helpful and professional staff.

Contents

Introduction

This is the second fat quarter book I have written for C&T Publishing. Instead of using all fat quarters, as I did in *Fat Quarter Winners*, I decided on a different approach—using one main background fabric and the rest fat quarters. I like this idea because it is easier to choose fabrics for the quilts, and it gives some consistency to the design. If you look at *Canasta* (page 11) and *Canfield* (page 16), you see that they are the same quilt, except *Canfield* is on point and uses a collection of fat quarters for backgrounds instead of one fabric. I wanted you to see how a scrappier background changes the look of the quilt. They are fun to make either way. You can use one consistent background or fat quarters; it's up to you!

I love to play cards—alone, with one other person, or with a group. The names of the quilts in the book are named after card games—just like in *Fat Quarter Winners*. This time I used the names of solitaire games as well. I love to play solitaire, especially on the computer.

The quilt *Spider* (page 32) is created with a square-in-a-square unit. Included in the directions are both the traditional instructions as well as the Fit to be Square Method. I designed the Fit to be Square ruler to trim Square-in-a-Square blocks without bias edges. The result of using this ruler is extremely accurate blocks.

Canasta, Canfield, Euchre, Pyramid, Baccarat, and *Poker* are quilts that use Flying Geese units. Included in the directions are both the traditional instructions as well as the Fit to be Geese Method. I also designed the Fit to be Geese ruler, and my goal was to accurately trim Flying Geese with very little waste. See Resources (page 63) for more on the Fit to be Square and Fit to be Geese rulers.

I hope that you enjoy making these quilts as much as my friends and I did.

General Instructions

This chapter contains the instructions for making the commonly used blocks in this book: combination units, half-square triangle units, Flying Geese units, and square-in-a-square units. The Flying Geese units and the square-in-a-square units can be made using either the traditional method or the Fit to be Geese or Fit to be Square rulers designed to help make these units (see Resources, page 63).

Combination Units

1. Sew a square to a rectangle as shown. Press in the direction of the arrows. Repeat to make a second square / rectangle unit. Rotate one unit and sew the two together as shown. Watch the placement of the square. On the back of the piece, snip ¼″ in the center of the seam allowance so that you can press half of the seam up and the other half down.

Snip.

2. On the back of a pieced rectangle, use the 45° mark on your ruler to draw 2 diagonal lines as shown. Note that the diagonal line should cross where your seams meet. Place the rectangle with the drawn lines right sides together on an unpieced rectangle. Sew exactly on the lines and cut ¼″ in from the lines. (Before cutting, check to make sure the sewn lines are in the correct direction.) Press in the direction of the arrows.

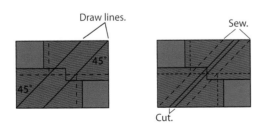

Draw lines.

Sew.

Cut.

Tip

Use the Fit to be Quarter ruler to trim pieces (see Resources, page 63). Refer to the instructions on the ruler package.

Half-Square Triangle Units

Draw a diagonal line from corner to corner on the back of the lighter square. Match the light square with a dark square, right sides together. Sew ¼″ from both sides of the line. Cut the pieces apart on the line, and press toward the darker triangle. Please note that in the instructions, half-square triangle units are made larger than needed so that you can square them to the exact size.

Draw line.   Sew.

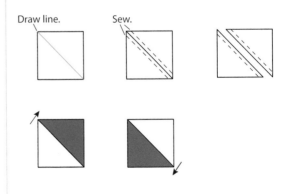

Flying Geese Units

Traditional Flying Geese Method

1. On the backs of 2 squares, draw a diagonal line from corner to corner.

Draw line.

2. Place a square on one end of the rectangle, right sides together. Sew directly on the line, and press in the direction of the arrow. You now have 3 layers of fabric in the corner. Trim the 2 underneath layers to ¼". Place the other square with a drawn line right sides together on the rectangle. The square will overlap the first square by ¼". Sew directly on the line, and press in the direction of the arrow. Trim the 2 underneath layers to ¼".

Fit to be Geese Method

1. Cut a square diagonally once to create 2 triangles.

2. Cut a square diagonally twice to create 4 triangles.

3. Sew the long side of a triangle from Step 1 to the short side of a triangle from Step 2. Press in the direction of the arrow. Sew a matching triangle from Step 1 to the other side of the triangle from Step 2. Press in the direction of the arrow.

4. Line up the rooftop of the Fit to be Geese ruler along the seam, as shown, and trim the top of the Flying Geese unit. Rotate the fabric 180° and line up the trimmed edge with the side of the Flying Geese unit that you are making. Trim the untrimmed edge.

5. Rotate the piece 90°. Align the trimmed top and bottom edges of the unit between the red lines for the correct size on the ruler. Make sure that the center red dotted line is lined up where the seams cross, and then trim. Use the dotted red line that is ¼" above the black line of the correct size.

6. Rotate the piece and trim the other side by again sandwiching the piece between the correct size and the red dotted line in the center.

Trim.

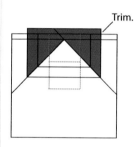

Trim.

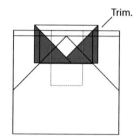

Trim.

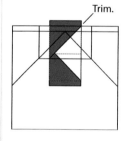

Trim.

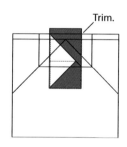

Square-in-a-Square Units

Traditional Square-in-a-Square Method

1. Cut 2 squares diagonally once to create 4 triangles.

2. Sew 2 triangles from Step 1 to the opposite sides of a square. Press toward the triangles. Sew 2 more of the triangles from Step 1 to the top and bottom of the square. Press toward the triangles.

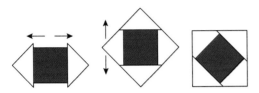

Fit to be Square Method

1. Cut 2 squares diagonally once to create 4 triangles.

2. Sew 2 triangles from Step 1 to the opposite sides of a square. Press toward the triangles. Sew 2 more of the triangles from Step 1 to the top and bottom of the square. Press toward the triangles.

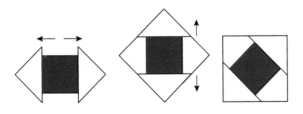

3. Line up the rooftop of the Fit to be Square ruler along the seam, making sure that the vertical line runs through the bottom seam where they cross, and trim the top of the square-in-a-square unit. Rotate the piece 180° and again line up the rooftop along the seam while lining up the cut edge along the correct block size. Trim. Rotate the piece 90°. Line up the rooftop along the seam and the vertical line on the bottom where the seams cross. Note that the sides should fall along the correct size for your block. Trim. Rotate 180°. Line up the rooftop, the bottom measurement, and the sides. Trim.

Trim.
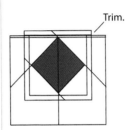

Trim.
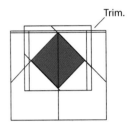

Trim.
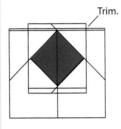

Trim.
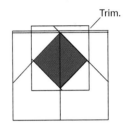

Solitaire

Designed and made by Monique Dillard
Quilted by LeAnne Olson

FINISHED BLOCK: 16″ × 16″
FINISHED QUILT: 64″ × 80″, 20 blocks

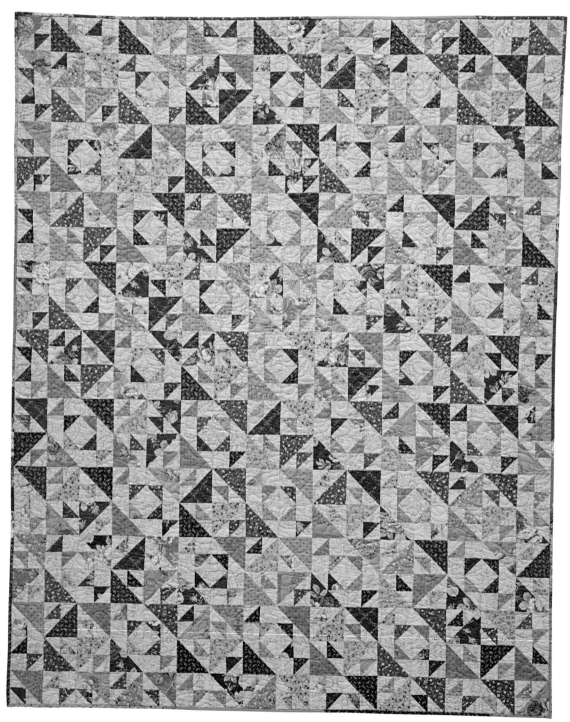

Information for making alternative quilt sizes is on page 10.

Materials

- Main light fabric: 3½ yards
- Dark fabric: 20 fat quarters (includes binding)
- Backing: 5 yards
- Batting: 74″ × 90″
- Optional: Fit to be Quarter ruler (page 63)

Cutting Instructions

Each fat quarter combined with the main light pieces is enough to make 1 block.

MAIN LIGHT

- Cut 20 strips 2½″ × width of fabric; cut into 240 pieces 2½″ × 3½″ (D).
- Cut 10 strips 2½″ × width of fabric; cut into 160 squares 2½″ × 2½″ (C).
- Cut 16 strips 3″ × width of fabric; cut into 200 squares 3″ × 3″ (A).

DARK FAT QUARTERS

- From each:

  Cut 1 strip 5½″ × width of fabric; cut into 4 pieces 4½″ × 5½″ (E).

  Cut 1 strip 6″ × width of fabric; cut into 2 pieces 4½″ × 5½″ (E) and 4 squares 3″ × 3″ (B).

  Cut 1 strip 3″ × width of fabric; cut into 6 squares 3″ × 3″ (B).

  Cut 1 strip 2¼″ × width of fabric for binding.

Piecing

1. Make 400 half-square triangle units (page 5) from each main light and dark using 200 light 3″ × 3″ squares (A) and 200 dark 3″ × 3″ squares (B). Press toward the dark. Trim the squares to 2½″ × 2½″.

Make 400 half-square triangles.

2. Sew 2 different half-square triangle units from Step 1 together with 2 main light 2½″ × 2½″ squares (C). Press in the direction of the arrows. Repeat to make 80.

Make 80.

3. Make 240 combination units (Refer to Combination Units, page 5) using 240 main light 2½″ × 3½″ pieces (D) and 240 half-square triangles from Step 2 and 2 dark fat quarters 4½″ × 5½″ pieces (E). Square to 4½″ × 4½″. Press

in the direction of the arrows. Watch the placement of the half-square triangles.

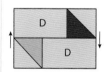

Make 120.

Make 240.

4. Sew 4 units from Step 3 together as shown in the diagram below. Press in the direction of the arrows. Square to 8½″ × 8½″. Repeat to make 40.

Make 40.

5. Sew 2 units from Step 2 and 2 units from Step 3 together as shown in the diagram below. Press in the direction of the arrows. Square to 8½″ × 8½″. Repeat to make 40.

Make 40.

6. Sew the units from Step 4 and Step 5 together as shown to make a block. Follow the diagram for placement. Press in the direction of the arrows. Square the block to 16½″ × 16½″.

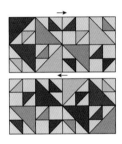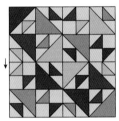

Make 20.

Repeat the entire procedure to make the number of blocks needed to complete your desired quilt size. (For a 64″ × 80″ quilt, page 8, make 20 blocks.)

Quilt Construction

Refer to the quilt photo on page 8 and the quilt assembly diagram. Follow the arrows for pressing direction.

1. Arrange and sew the quilt in rows.

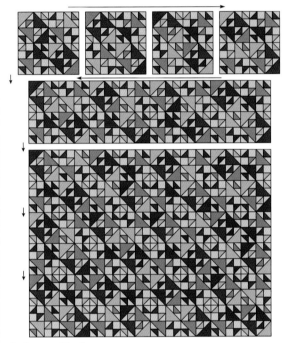

Quilt assembly diagram

2. Quilt, bind, and enjoy! (See Quiltmaking Basics, page 61.)

ALTERNATIVE QUILT SIZES	TWIN	FULL / QUEEN	KING
Number of blocks	24	42	49
Number of blocks, wide by long	4 × 6	6 × 7	7 × 7
Finished size	64″ × 96″	96″ × 112″	112″ × 112″
YARDAGE			
Main light	4⅓ yards	7½ yards	8⅔ yards
Dark fat quarters (includes binding)	24	42	49
Backing	5⅞ yards	9 yards	10¼ yards
Batting	74″ × 106″	106″ × 122″	122″ × 122″
MAIN LIGHT CUTTING	CUT THE STRIPS, AND FROM THOSE STRIPS CUT THE SMALLER PIECES.		
Number of strips × width of fabric Number of pieces (D)	24–2½″ strips 288–2½″ × 3½″	42–2½″ strips 504–2½″ × 3½″	49–2½″ strips 588–2½″ × 3½″
Number of strips × width of fabric Number of squares (C)	12–2½″ strips 192–2½″ × 2½″	21–2½″ strips 336–2½″ × 2½″	25–2½″ strips 392–2½″ × 2½″
Number of strips × width of fabric Number of squares (A)	19–3″ strips 240–3″ × 3″	33–3″ strips 420–3″ × 3″	38–3″ strips 490–3″ × 3″

Canasta

Designed by Monique Dillard
Made and quilted by Sue Glorch

FINISHED BLOCK: 8″ × 8″
FINISHED QUILT: 55″ × 71″, 35 blocks

Information for making alternative quilt sizes is on page 15.

Materials

- Main light fabric: 2⅛ yards
- Medium fabric: 6 fat quarters
- Dark fabric: 6 fat quarters
- First border: ½ yard
- Second border: ½ yard
- Third border: 1¼ yards
- Binding: ⅝ yard
- Backing: 4 yards
- Batting: 65″ × 81″
- Optional: Fit to be Geese ruler (page 63)

Cutting Instructions

Before cutting, match your medium and dark fat quarters into pairs for piecing. Cut the fat quarters separately. Piece the blocks using a medium and dark fat quarter combination and the main light. Each fat quarter combination makes 3 dark blocks and 3 light blocks.

MAIN LIGHT

Fit to be Geese Method (page 6)

- Cut 3 strips 5½″ × width of fabric; cut into 18 squares 5½″ × 5½″, and cut diagonally twice to make 72 triangles (B).
- Cut 6 strips 3¼″ × width of fabric; cut into 72 squares 3¼″ × 3¼″, and cut diagonally once to make 144 triangles (C).

- Cut 12 strips 1½″ × width of fabric; cut into 24 pieces 1½″ × 20″.
- Cut 3 strips 2½″ × width of fabric; cut into 6 pieces 2½″ × 20″.

OR

Traditional Flying Geese Method (page 6)

- Cut 9 strips 2½″ × width of fabric; cut into 144 squares 2½″ × 2½″ (C).
- Cut 5 strips 4½″ × width of fabric; cut into 72 pieces 4½″ × 2½″ (B).
- Cut 12 strips 1½″ × width of fabric; cut into 24 pieces 1½″ × 20″.
- Cut 3 strips 2½″ × width of fabric; cut into 6 pieces 2½″ × 20″.

MEDIUM FAT QUARTERS

- From each:

  Cut 1 strip 2½″ × width of fabric.

  Cut 6 strips 1½″ × width of fabric.

DARK FAT QUARTERS

Fit to be Geese Method (page 6)

- From each:

  Cut 1 strip 5½″ × width of fabric; cut into 3 squares 5½″ × 5½″, and cut diagonally twice to make 12 triangles (D).

  Cut 2 strips 3¼″ × width of fabric; cut into 12 squares 3¼″ × 3¼″, and cut diagonally once to make 24 triangles (A).

  Cut 2 strips 1½″ × width of fabric.

OR

Traditional Flying Geese Method (page 6)

- From each:

  Cut 4 strips 2½″ × width of fabric; cut into 24 squares 2½″ × 2½″ (A) and 4 pieces 2½″ × 4½″ (D).

  Cut 1 strip 4½″ × width of fabric; cut into 8 pieces 2½″ × 4½″ (D).

  Cut 2 strips 1½″ × width of fabric.

FIRST BORDER

- Cut 6 strips 2″ × width of fabric.

SECOND BORDER

- Cut 6 strips 1½″ × width of fabric.

THIRD BORDER

- Cut 7 strips 5½″ × width of fabric.

BINDING

- Cut 7 strips 2½″ × width of fabric.

Piecing

1. Sew a dark strip 1½″ × width of fabric to a medium strip 1½″ × width of fabric. Press toward the dark. Repeat to make 2 sets. Cut into 24 segments 1½″ wide. Rotate 1 segment and sew together in pairs to make 12 Four-Patches. Press in the direction of the arrow.

1½″

Make 12.

2. Sew a medium strip 1½″ × width of fabric to a main light 1½″ × 20″ piece. Press toward the medium. Repeat to make 2 sets. Cut into 24 segments 1½″ wide. Rotate 1 segment and sew together in pairs to make 12 Four-Patches. Press in the direction of the arrow.

1½″

Make 12.

3. Sew a medium strip 1½″ × width of fabric to both sides of a main light 2½″ × 20″ piece. Press toward the medium. Cut into 12 segments 1½″ wide.

1½″

Cut into 12 segments.

4. Sew a main light 1½″ × 20″ piece to both sides of a medium strip 2½″ × width of fabric. Press toward the medium. Cut into 6 segments 2½″ wide.

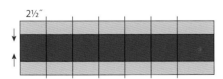

2½″

Cut into 6 segments.

5. Sew a piece from Step 3 to both sides of a piece from Step 4. Press in the direction of the arrows. Repeat to make 6. Square to 4½″ × 4½″.

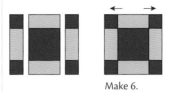

Make 6.

6. Make 12 Flying Geese units (page 6) measuring 2½″ × 4½″ from the main light and dark fat quarter.

For the Fit to be Geese Method (page 6), use 24 dark triangles cut from 3¼″ × 3¼″ squares cut diagonally once (A) and 12 main light triangles cut from 5½″ × 5½″ squares cut diagonally twice (B).

OR

For the Traditional Flying Geese Method (page 6), use 24 dark 2½″ × 2½″ squares (A) and 12 main light 2½″ × 4½″ pieces (B).

Make 12.

7. Make 12 Flying Geese units measuring 2½″ × 4½″ from the dark fat quarter and main light.

For the Fit to be Geese Method, use 24 main light triangles cut from 3¼″ × 3¼″ squares cut diagonally once (C) and 12 dark triangles cut from 5½″ × 5½″ squares cut diagonally twice (D).

OR

For the Traditional Flying Geese Method, use 24 main light 2½″ × 2½″ squares (C) and 12 dark 2½″ × 4½″ pieces (D).

Make 12.

8. Construct a dark block using the pieces from Step 1, Step 5, and Step 6. Press in the direction of the arrows.

Square the block to 8½″ × 8½″. Repeat to make 3 dark blocks per dark and medium fat quarter combination for your desired quilt size. (For a 55″ × 71″ quilt, page 11, make 18 dark blocks.)

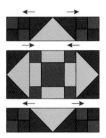
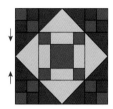

Make 3 dark blocks.

9. Construct a light block using the pieces from Step 2, Step 5, and Step 7. Press in the direction of the arrows. Square the block to 8½″ × 8½″. Repeat to make 3 light blocks per dark and medium fat quarter combination for the total number of blocks needed to complete your desired quilt size. (For a 55″ × 71″ quilt, page 11, make 18 light blocks; you will use only 17.)

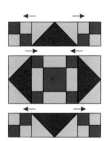
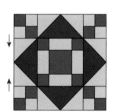

Make 3 light blocks.

Quilt Construction

Refer to the quilt photo on page 11 and the quilt assembly diagram.

1. Arrange and sew your quilt in rows. Press in the direction of the arrows.

2. Sew on the first border, the second border, and the third border (see Quiltmaking Basics, page 61). Press toward the borders.

Quilt assembly diagram

3. Quilt, bind, and enjoy! (See Quiltmaking Basics, page 61.)

ALTERNATIVE QUILT SIZES	TWIN	FULL / QUEEN	KING
Number of blocks	45	99	144
Number of blocks, wide × long	5 × 9	9 × 11	12 × 12
Finished size	57" × 89"	89" × 105"	113" × 113"
YARDAGE			
Main light	2¾ yards	5⅝ yards	7¾ yards
Medium fat quarters	8	17	24
Dark fat quarters	8	17	24
First border	½ yard	⅝ yard	¾ yard
Second border	⅓ yard	½ yard	⅝ yard
Third border	1½ yards*	2 yards*	2¼ yards*
Binding	¾ yard	⅞ yard	1 yard
Backing	5½ yards	8¼ yards	10¼ yards
Batting	67" × 99"	99" × 115"	123" × 123"
MAIN LIGHT CUTTING FIT TO BE GEESE METHOD	CUT THE STRIPS, AND FROM THOSE STRIPS CUT THE SMALLER PIECES.		
Number of strips × width of fabric Number of squares–cut diagonally twice (B) triangles	4–5½" strips 23–5½" × 5½"	8–5½" strips 50–5½" × 5½"	11–5½" strips 72–5½" × 5½"
Number of strips × width of fabric Number of squares–cut diagonally once (C) triangles	8–3¼" strips 92–3¼" × 3¼"	17–3¼" strips 200–3¼" × 3¼"	24–3¼" strips 288–3¼" × 3¼"
Number of strips × width of fabric Number of pieces	16–1½" strips 32–1½" × 20"	34–1½" strips 68–1½" × 20"	48–1½" strips 96–1½" × 20"
Number of strips × width of fabric Number of pieces	4–2½" strips 8–2½" × 20"	9–2½" strips 17–2½" × 20"	12–2½" strips 24–2½" × 20"
MAIN LIGHT CUTTING TRADITIONAL FLYING GEESE METHOD	CUT THE STRIPS, AND FROM THOSE STRIPS CUT THE SMALLER PIECES.		
Number of strips × width of fabric Number of pieces (B)	6–4½" strips 92–4½" × 2½"	13–4½" strips 200–4½" × 2½"	18–4½" strips 288–4½" × 2½"
Number of strips × width of fabric Number of squares (C)	12–2½" strips 184–2½" × 2½"	25–2½" strips 400–2½" × 2½"	36–2½" strips 576–2½" × 2½"
Number of strips × width of fabric Number of pieces	16–1½" strips 32–1½" × 20"	34–1½" strips 68–1½" × 20"	48–1½" strips 96–1½" × 20"
Number of strips × width of fabric Number of pieces	4–2½" strips 8–2½" × 20"	9–2½" strips 17–2½" × 20"	12–2½" strips 24–2½" × 20"

*For these larger sizes, cut the outer border 6½".

Canfield

Designed and made by Monique Dillard
Quilted by LeAnne Olson

FINISHED BLOCK: 8″ × 8″
FINISHED QUILT: 47″ × 47″, 13 blocks,
8 half blocks, 4 quarter blocks

Note: This quilt is not like the others. It uses fat quarter backgrounds to create a scrappy look.

Materials

- Light fabric: 5 fat quarters

- Medium fabric: 5 fat quarters

- Dark fabric: 5 fat quarters

- First border and third border: ½ yard

- Second border: 1 yard

- Binding: ½ yard

- Backing: 3¼ yards

- Batting: 57″ × 57″

- Optional: Fit to be Geese ruler (page 63)

Cutting Instructions

Before cutting, match your light, medium, and dark fat quarters into sets for piecing. Cut the fat quarters separately. Each set of fat quarters makes 2 dark blocks, 1 light block, 2 half blocks, and 1 quarter block.

LIGHT FAT QUARTERS
Fit to be Geese Method (page 6)

- From each:

  Cut 1 strip 5½″ × width of fabric; cut into 2 squares 5½″ × 5½″, and cut diagonally twice to make 8 triangles (E). Also cut 8 pieces 1½″ × 2½″ (B) from the same strip.

Cut 2 strips 3¼″ × width of fabric; cut into 9 squares 3¼″ × 3¼″, and cut diagonally once to make 18 triangles (F).

Cut 2 strips 1½″ × width of fabric.

Cut 1 strip 2½″ × width of fabric.

OR

Traditional Flying Geese Method (page 6)

- From each:

  Cut 5 strips 2½″ × width of fabric; cut into 8 pieces 2½″ × 4½″ (E), 18 pieces 2½″ × 2½″ (F), and 8 pieces 1½″ × 2½″ (B).

  Cut 2 strips 1½″ × width of fabric.

  Cut 1 strip 2½″ × width of fabric.

MEDIUM FAT QUARTERS

- From each:

  Cut 1 strip 2½″ × width of fabric; cut into 6 squares 2½″ × 2½″ (C).

  Cut 6 strips 1½″ × width of fabric; cut 1 strip into 8 squares 1½″ × 1½″ (A).

DARK FAT QUARTERS
Fit to be Geese Method

- From each:

  Cut 1 strip 5½″ × width of fabric; cut into 3 squares 5½″ × 5½″, and cut diagonally twice to make 12 triangles (G).

Cut 2 strips 3¼″ × width of fabric; cut into 8 squares 3¼″ × 3¼″, and cut diagonally once to make 16 triangles (D).

Cut 2 strips 1½″ × width of fabric.

OR

Traditional Flying Geese Method

- From each:

  Cut 5 strips 2½″ × width of fabric; cut into 9 pieces 4½″ × 2½″ (G) and 8 squares 2½″ × 2½″ (D).

  Cut 2 strips 1½″ × width of fabric.

FIRST BORDER

- Cut 4 strips 1½″ × width of fabric.

SECOND BORDER

- Cut 5 strips 5″ × width of fabric.

THIRD BORDER

- Cut 5 strips 1½″ × width of fabric.

BINDING

- Cut 5 strips 2¼″ × width of fabric.

Piecing

1. Sew a dark strip 1½″ × width of fabric to a medium strip 1½″ × width of fabric. Press toward the dark. Repeat to make 2 sets. Cut into 16 segments 1½″ wide. Rotate 1 piece and sew together to make 8 Four-Patches. Press in the direction of the arrow.

Make 8.

2. Sew a medium strip 1½″ × width of fabric to a light strip 1½″ × width of fabric. Press toward the medium. Repeat to make 2 sets. Cut into 18 segments 1½″ wide. Rotate 1 piece and sew together to make 6 Four-Patches. Press in the direction of the arrow. (You will have 6 segments left over to use in Step 3.)

Make 6.

3. Sew the leftover segments from Step 2 with a medium 1½″ × 1½″ square (A) as shown. Press in the direction of the arrow. Repeat to make 6. (These segments will be used in Steps 14 and 15.)

Make 6.

4. Sew a medium strip 1½″ × width of fabric to both sides of a light strip 2½″ × width of fabric. Press toward the medium. Cut into 9 segments 1½″ wide. (You will use 6 segments for Step 6, 2 segments for Step 8, and 1 segment for Step 9.)

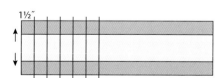

Cut into 9 segments.

5. Sew a light 1½″ × 2½″ piece (B) to both sides of a medium 2½″ × 2½″ square (C). Press toward the medium. Repeat to make 3.

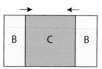

Make 3.

6. Sew a piece from Step 4 to both sides of the piece from Step 5. Press in the direction of the arrows. Repeat to make 3.

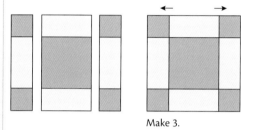

Make 3.

7. Sew a light 1½″ × 2½″ piece (B) to a medium 2½″ × 2½″ square (C). Press toward the medium. Repeat to make 2.

Make 2.

8. Sew a piece from Step 4 to the top of the piece from Step 7 and a medium 1½″ × 1½″ square (A) to the bottom as shown. Press in the direction of the arrows. Repeat to make 2 for half blocks.

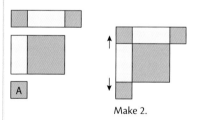

Make 2.

9. Sew a piece from Step 4 to a medium 2½" × 2½" square (C). Press toward the medium square.

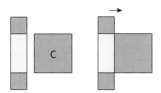

Make 1 for quarter block.

10. Make 8 Flying Geese units (page 6) measuring 2½" × 4½" using the light and dark fat quarters.

For the Fit to be Geese Method (page 6), use 16 dark triangles cut from 3¼" × 3¼" squares cut diagonally once (D) and 8 light triangles cut from 5½" × 5½" squares cut diagonally twice (E).

OR

For the Traditional Flying Geese Method (page 6), use 16 dark 2½" × 2½" squares (D) and 8 light 2½" × 4½" pieces (E).

Make 8.

11. Make 12 Flying Geese units measuring 2½" × 4½" from the dark fat quarter and light fat quarter.

For the Fit to be Geese Method, use 18 light triangles cut from 3¼" × 3¼" squares cut diagonally once (F) and 9 dark triangles cut from 5½" × 5½" squares cut diagonally twice (G).

OR

For the Traditional Flying Geese Method, use 18 light 2½" × 2½" squares (F) and 9 dark fat quarter 2½" × 4½" pieces (G).

Make 9 for light block, half blocks, and quarter block.

12. Construct a dark block using the pieces from Step 1, Step 6, and Step 10. Press in the direction of the arrows. Square the block to 8½" × 8½". Repeat to make 2 dark blocks per light, dark, and medium fat quarter combination for a total of 10 blocks. (You will have an extra block.)

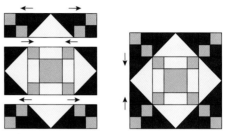

Make 2 dark blocks from each color combination.

13. Construct the light block using the pieces from Step 2, Step 6, and Step 11. Press in the direction of the arrows. Square the block to 8½" × 8½". Repeat to make 1 light block per light, dark, and medium fat quarter combination for a total of 5 blocks. (You will have an extra block.)

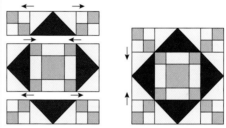

Make 1 light block from each color combination.

14. Sew the pieces from Step 2, Step 3, Step 8, and Step 11 together to make a half block as shown. Press in the direction of the arrows. Repeat to make 2 half blocks per light, medium, and dark fat quarter combination to make a total of 10 half blocks. (You will have 2 extra half blocks.)

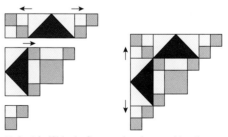

Make 2 half blocks from each color combination.

15. Sew the pieces from Step 3, Step 9, and Step 11 together to make a quarter block as shown. Press in the direction of the arrow. Make 1 quarter block per light, medium and dark fat quarter combination to make a total of 5 quarter blocks. (You will have an extra block.)

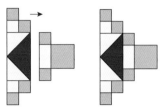

Make 1 quarter block per color combination.

Quilt Construction

Refer to the quilt photo on page 16 and the quilt assembly diagram.

1. Arrange and sew your quilt in rows. Press in the direction of the arrows.

2. Trim the quilt to ¼″ from the seam. Sew on the first border, the second border, and the third border (see Quiltmaking Basics, on page 61). Press toward the borders.

Tip

Use spray starch to keep the edges from fraying when you trim and before you sew on your borders.

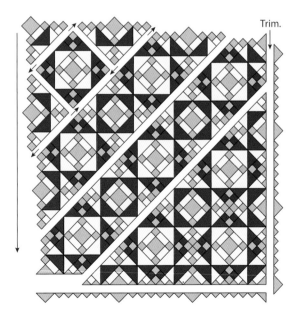
Trim.

Quilt assembly diagram

3. Quilt, bind, and enjoy! (See Quiltmaking Basics, page 61.)

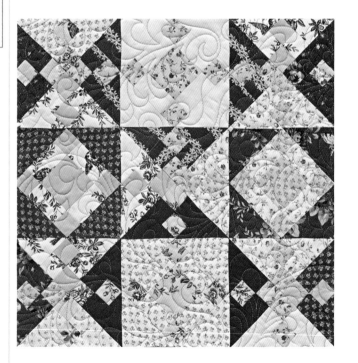

Euchre

Designed and made by Monique Dillard
Quilted by Danette Gonzalez

FINISHED BLOCK: 9″ × 9″
FINISHED QUILT: 45″ × 63″, 35 blocks

Information for making alternative quilt sizes is on page 25.

Materials

- Main light fabric: 2⅞ yards
- Blue fabric: 9 fat quarters
- Red fabric: 5 fat quarters
- Backing: 3⅛ yards
- Batting: 55″ × 73″
- Optional: Fit to be Geese ruler (page 63)

Cutting Instructions

Before beginning, match 1 red with 2 blues into sets for piecing. You will have a set of red pieces left over. Cut the fat quarters separately. Each set of blue and half of the red pieces, along with the main light, make 4 blocks. You will have a block left over.

MAIN LIGHT
Fit to be Geese Method (page 6)

- Cut 4 strips 4½″ × width of fabric; cut into 36 squares 4½″ × 4½″, and cut diagonally twice to make 144 triangles (D).

- Cut 8 strips 3½″ × width of fabric; cut into 144 pieces 3½″ × 2″ (E).

- Cut 10 strips 2¾″ × width of fabric; cut into 144 squares 2¾″ × 2¾″, and cut diagonally once to make 288 triangles (A).

- Cut 9 strips 2″ × width of fabric; cut into 18 pieces 2″ × 20″.

OR

Traditional Flying Geese Method (page 6)

- Cut 12 strips 2″ × width of fabric; cut into 144 pieces 2″ × 3½″ (D).

- Cut 8 strips 3½″ × width of fabric; cut into 144 pieces 3½″ × 2″ (E).

- Cut 14 strips 2″ × width of fabric; cut into 288 squares 2″ × 2″ (A).

- Cut 9 strips 2″ × width of fabric; cut into 18 pieces 2″ × 20″.

BLUE FAT QUARTERS
Fit to be Geese Method (page 6)

- From each:

  Cut 1 strip 4½″ × width of fabric; cut into 4 squares 4½″ × 4½″, and cut each diagonally twice to make 16 triangles (B).

  Cut 3 strips 2¾″ × width of fabric; cut into 16 squares 2¾″ × 2¾″, and cut each diagonally once to make 32 triangles (C).

  Cut 2 strips 2″ × width of fabric.

OR

Traditional Flying Geese Method (page 6)

- From each:

  Cut 6 strips 2″ × width of fabric; cut into 16 pieces 2″ × 3½″ (B) and 32 squares 2″ × 2″ (C).

  Cut 2 strips 2″ × width of fabric.

RED FAT QUARTERS

- From each:

  Cut 4 strips 2″ × width of fabric.

  Cut 3 strips 2¼″ × width of fabric for binding.

Piecing

1. Make 16 Flying Geese units measuring 2″ × 3½″ from the main light and blue fat quarters in each fabric combination.

For the Fit to be Geese Method (page 6), use 32 main light triangles cut from 2¾″ × 2¾″ squares cut diagonally once (A) and 16 blue fat quarter triangles cut from 4½″ × 4½″ squares cut diagonally twice (B).

OR

For the Traditional Flying Geese Method (page 6), use 32 main light 2″ × 2″ squares (A) and 16 blue fat quarter 2″ × 3½″ pieces (B).

Make 16 from each blue fat quarter.

2. Make 16 Flying Geese units measuring 2″ × 3½″ from the blue fat quarters and main light in each fabric combination.

For the Fit to be Geese Method (page 6), use 32 blue fat quarter triangles cut from 2¾″ × 2¾″ squares cut diagonally once (C) and 16 main light triangles cut from 4½″ × 4½″ squares cut diagonally twice (D).

OR

For the Traditional Flying Geese Method (page 6), use 32 blue fat quarter 2″ × 2″ squares (C) and 16 main light 2″ × 3½″ pieces (D).

Make 16 from each blue fat quarter.

3. Sew the pieces from Steps 1 and 2 together as shown. Press in the direction of the arrows. Square to 3½″ × 3½″. Repeat to make 16 from each blue fat quarter.

Make 16 from each blue fat quarter.

4. Sew a main light 2″ × 20″ piece to a red fat quarter strip 2″ × width of fabric. Press in the direction of the arrow. Cut into 8 segments 2″ wide.

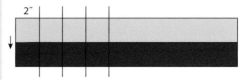

Cut into 8 segments.

5. Sew a piece from Step 4 to a main light 2″ × 3½″ piece (E). Press in the direction of the arrow. Square to 3½″ × 3½″. Repeat to make 8.

Make 8.

6. Sew a blue fat quarter strip 2″ × width of fabric to a main light 2″ × 20″ piece. Press in the direction of the arrow. Cut into 8 segments 2″ wide.

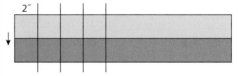

Cut into 8 segments.

7. Sew a piece from Step 6 to a main light 2″ × 3½″ piece (E). Press in the direction of the arrow. Square to 3½″ × 3½″. Repeat to make 8.

Make 8.

8. Sew a blue fat quarter strip 2″ × width of fabric to a red fat quarter strip 2″ × width of fabric. Press in the direction of the arrow. Cut into 8 pieces 2″ wide. Rotate 1 piece and sew to another to make a Four-Patch. Repeat to make 4 per red-and-blue set.

Make 4.

9. Sew the block together using the pieces from Step 3, Step 5, Step 7, and Step 8. Press in the direction of the arrows. Square to 9½″ × 9½″. Repeat to make 4 blocks per red-and-blue fat quarter set for the total number of blocks needed to complete your desired quilt size. (For the 45″ × 63″ quilt, page 21, make 35 blocks. You will have an extra block.)

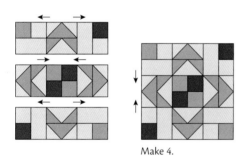

Make 4.

Quilt Construction

Refer to the quilt photo on page 21 and the quilt assembly diagram. Follow the arrows for pressing direction.

1. Arrange and sew the quilt in rows.

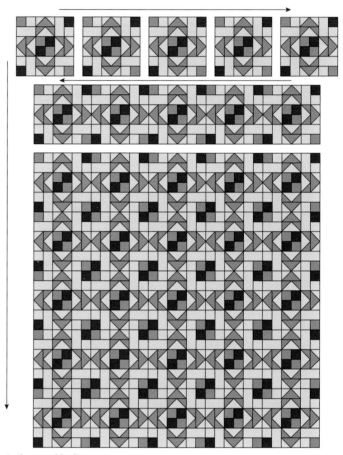

Quilt assembly diagram

2. Quilt, bind, and enjoy! (See Quiltmaking Basics, page 61.)

ALTERNATIVE QUILT SIZES	TWIN	FULL / QUEEN	KING
Number of blocks	70*	120	144
Number of blocks, wide × long	7 × 10	10 × 12	12 × 12
Finished size	63″ × 90″	90″ × 108″	108″ × 108″
YARDAGE			
Main light	5½ yards	9 yards	10¾ yards
Red fat quarters	9	15	18
Blue fat quarters	18	30	36
Backing	5¾ yards	8⅜ yards	9⅞ yards
Batting	73″ × 100″	100″ × 118″	118″ × 118″
MAIN LIGHT CUTTING FIT TO BE GEESE METHOD	CUT THE STRIPS, AND FROM THOSE STRIPS CUT THE SMALLER PIECES.		
Number of strips × width of fabric Number of squares–cut diagonally twice (D) triangles	8–4½″ strips 70–4½″ × 4½″	14–4½″ strips 120–4½″ × 4½″	16–4½″ strips 144–4½″ × 4½″
Number of strips × width of fabric Number of squares–cut diagonally once (A) triangles	20–2¾″ strips 280–2¾″ × 2¾″	35–2¾″ strips 480–2¾″ × 2¾″	42–2¾″ strips 576–2¾″ × 2¾″
Number of strips × width of fabric Number of pieces (E)	24–2″ strips 280–2″ × 3½″	40–2″ strips 480–2″ × 3½″	48–2″ strips 576–2″ × 3½″
Number of strips × width of fabric Number of pieces	18–2″ strips 36–2″ × 20″	30–2″ strips 60–2″ × 20″	36–2″ strips 72–2″ × 20″
MAIN LIGHT CUTTING TRADITIONAL FLYING GEESE METHOD	CUT THE STRIPS, AND FROM THOSE STRIPS CUT THE SMALLER PIECES.		
Number of strips × width of fabric Number of pieces (D)	24–2″ strips 280–2″ × 3½″	40–2″ strips 480–2″ × 3½″	48–2″ strips 576–2″ × 3½″
Number of strips × width of fabric Number of squares (A)	28–2″ strips 560–2″ × 2″	48–2″ strips 960–2″ × 2″	58–2″ strips 1,152–2″ × 2″
Number of strips × width of fabric Number of pieces (E)	24–2″ strips 280–2″ × 3½″	40–2″ strips 480–2″ × 3½″	48–2″ strips 576–2″ × 3½″
Number of strips × width of fabric Number of pieces	18–2″ strips 36–2″ × 20″	30–2″ strips 60–2″ × 20″	36–2″ strips 72–2″ × 20″

*You will have 2 extra blocks.

Pyramid

Designed by Monique Dillard
Made by Joyce Davis
Quilted by LeAnne Olson

FINISHED BLOCK: 9″ × 9″
FINISHED QUILT: 61½″ × 72″, 20 blocks

Information for making alternative quilt sizes is on page 31.

Materials

- Main light fabric: 2 yards
- Brown fabric: 4 fat quarters
- Red fabric: 4 fat quarters
- Blue fabric: 4 fat quarters
- Inner border: ½ yard
- Outer border: 1½ yards
- Binding: ⅔ yard
- Backing: 4 yards
- Batting: 72″ × 82″
- Optional: Fit to be Geese ruler (page 63)

Cutting Instructions

Before beginning, match brown, red, and blue fat quarters into sets for piecing. Cut the brown, red, and blue fat quarters separately. Each set of fat quarters, along with the main light, makes 5 blocks.

MAIN LIGHT
Fit to be Geese Method (page 6)

- Cut 3 strips 4½″ × width of fabric; cut into 20 squares 4½″ × 4½″, and cut diagonally twice to make 80 triangles (B).

- Cut 24 strips 2″ × width of fabric; cut into 16 pieces 2″ × 21″ for strip piecing, 49 pieces 2″ × 9½″ (I), 18 pieces 2″ × 6½″ (G), and 22 squares 2″ × 2″ (H).

OR

Traditional Flying Geese Method (page 6)

- Cut 32 strips 2″ × width of fabric; cut into 16 pieces 2″ × 20″ for strip piecing, 49 pieces 2″ × 9½″ (I), 18 pieces 2″ × 6½″ (G), 80 pieces 2″ × 3½″ (B), and 22 squares 2″ × 2″ (H).

BROWN FAT QUARTERS
Fit to be Geese Method (page 6)

- From each:

  Cut 1 strip 4½″ × width of fabric; cut into 4 squares 4½″ × 4½″, and cut each diagonally twice to make 16 triangles (D).

  Cut 2 strips 2¾″ × width of fabric; cut into 14 squares 2¾″ × 2¾″, and cut diagonally once to make 28 triangles (A).

  Cut 1 strip 5½″ × width of fabric; cut into 1 square 4½″ × 4½″ and 6 squares 2¾″ × 2¾″. Cut the 4½″ × 4½″ squares diagonally twice to make 4 triangles (D), and cut the 2¾″ × 2¾″ squares diagonally once to make 12 triangles (A).

OR

Traditional Flying Geese Method (page 6)

- From each:

  Cut 8 strips 2″ × width of fabric; cut into 20 pieces 2″ × 3½″ (D) and 40 squares 2″ × 2″ (A).

RED FAT QUARTERS

- From each:

  Cut 1 strip 3½″ × width of fabric; cut into 5 squares 3½″ × 3½″ (E).

  Cut 4 strips 2″ × width of fabric; cut into 18 squares 2″ × 2″ (F); reserve 2 strips 2″ × width of fabric for strip piecing.

BLUE FAT QUARTERS
Fit to be Geese Method (page 6)

- From each:

  Cut 3 strips 2¾″ × width of fabric; cut into 20 squares 2¾″ × 2¾″, and cut diagonally once to make 40 triangles (C).

  Cut 2 strips 2″ × width of fabric for strip piecing.

OR

Traditional Flying Geese Method (page 6)

- From each:

  Cut 6 strips 2″ × width of fabric; cut 4 strips into 40 squares 2″ × 2″ (C); reserve the last 2 strips 2″ × width of fabric for strip piecing.

INNER BORDER
- Cut 6 strips 2″ × width of fabric.

OUTER BORDER
- Cut 7 strips 6½″ × width of fabric.

BINDING
- Cut 8 strips 2½″ × width of fabric.

Piecing

1. Make 20 Flying Geese units measuring 2″ × 3½″ from the main light and brown fat quarters in each fabric combination.

For the Fit to be Geese Method (page 6), use 40 brown fat quarter triangles cut from 2¾″ × 2¾″ squares cut diagonally once (A) and 20 main light triangles cut from 4½″ × 4½″ squares cut diagonally twice (B).

OR

For the Traditional Flying Geese Method (page 6), use 40 brown fat quarter 2″ × 2″ squares (A) and 20 main light 2″ × 3½″ pieces (B).

Make 20 from each main light and brown fat quarter pair.

2. Make 20 Flying Geese units measuring 2″ × 3½″ from the brown fat quarters and blue fat quarters in each fabric combination.

For the Fit to be Geese Method (page 6), use 40 blue fat quarter triangles cut from 2¾″ × 2¾″ squares cut diagonally once (C) and 20 brown triangles cut from 4½″ × 4½″ squares cut diagonally twice (D).

OR

For the Traditional Flying Geese Method (page 6), use 40 blue fat quarter 2″ × 2″ squares (C) and 20 brown 2″ × 3½″ pieces (D).

Make 20 from each blue and brown fat quarter pair.

3. Sew the pieces from Steps 1 and 2 together as shown. Make sure that you match your brown fat quarter fabric. Press in the direction of the arrows. Square to 3½″ × 3½″.

Repeat to make 20 from each main light, brown, and blue combination.

Make 20 from each color combination.

4. Sew a main light 2″ × 21″ piece to a red fat quarter strip 2″ × width of fabric. Make 2 per red fat quarter. Press in the direction of the arrow. Cut into 10 pieces 2″ wide per strip set for a total of 20.

Make 2 per red fat quarter and main light.
Cut into 10 pieces 2″ wide per strip set for total of 20.

5. Sew a main light 2″ × 21″ piece to a blue fat quarter strip 2″ × width of fabric. Make 2 per blue fat quarter. Press in the direction of the arrow. Cut into 10 pieces 2″ wide per strip set for a total of 20.

Make 2 per blue fat quarter and main light.
Cut into 10 pieces 2″ wide per strip set for total of 20.

6. Sew the pieces from Steps 4 and 5 together to make a Four-Patch. Press in the direction of the arrow. Square to 3½″ × 3½″. Make 20 per main light, red, and blue combination.

Make 20 from each color combination.

7. Sew the block together using the pieces from Step 3, the Four-Patches from Step 6, and the matching red 3½″ × 3½″ square (E). Press in the direction of the arrows. Square to 9½″ × 9½″. Repeat to make 5 blocks per red, blue, brown, and main light color combination for the total number of blocks needed to complete your desired quilt size. (For the 61½″ × 72″ quilt, page 26, make 20 blocks.)

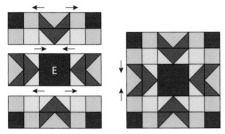

Make 5 blocks from each color combination.

8. On the ends of the main light 2″ × 6½″ piece (G), sew a red 2″ × 2″ square (F). Use various reds to make it scrappy. Press toward the red squares. Repeat to make 18.

Make 18.

9. Sew a top piece together by using 2 red 2″ × 2″ squares (F), 5 main light 2″ × 2″ squares (H), and 4 pieces from Step 8. Press in the direction of the arrows. Repeat to make another exactly the same for the bottom piece of the quilt.

Make 1 for top and 1 for bottom of quilt.

10. Sew a sashing row together using 2 main light 2″ × 2″ squares (H), 5 red 2″ × 2″ squares (F), and 4 main light 2″ × 9½″ pieces (I). Press in the direction of the arrows. Repeat to make 6.

Make 6.

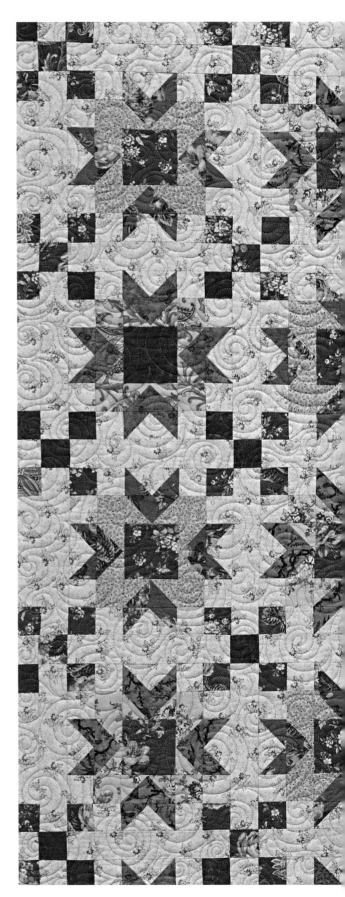

Quilt Construction

Refer to the quilt photo on page 26 and the quilt assembly diagram.

1. Arrange and sew together the quilt in rows with a main light 2" × 9½" piece (I) between the blocks and a piece from Step 8 on each end of the row. The top and bottom pieces from Step 9 should be at the top and bottom, and the sashing pieces from Step 10 should be between the rows. Press in the direction of the arrows.

2. Sew on the inner border and the outer borders (see Quiltmaking Basics, page 61). Press toward the borders.

Quilt assembly diagram

3. Quilt, bind, and enjoy! (See Quiltmaking Basics, page 61.)

ALTERNATIVE QUILT SIZES	TWIN	FULL / QUEEN	KING
Number of blocks*	28	56	81
Number of blocks, wide × long	4 × 7	7 × 8	9 × 9
Finished size	61½″ × 93″	93″ × 103½″	114″ × 114″
YARDAGE			
Main light	2¾ yards	4¾ yards	6⅝ yards
Brown fat quarters	6	12	17
Red fat quarters	6	12	17
Blue fat quarters	6	12	17
Inner border	½ yard	⅝ yard	⅔ yard
Outer border	1⅔ yards	2 yards	2⅜ yards
Binding	¾ yard	⅞ yard	1 yard
Backing	5¾ yards	8⅝ yards	10⅓ yards
Batting	72″ × 103″	103″ × 114″	124″ × 124″

MAIN LIGHT CUTTING FIT TO BE GEESE METHOD

CUT THE STRIPS, AND FROM THOSE STRIPS CUT THE SMALLER PIECES.

	TWIN	FULL / QUEEN	KING
Number of strips × width of fabric Number of squares–cut diagonally twice (B) triangles	4–4½″ strips 28–4½″ × 4½″	7–4½″ strips 56–4½″ × 4½″	9–4½″ strips 81–4½″ × 4½″
Number of strips × width of fabric Number of pieces	12–2″ strips 24–2″ × 20″	24–2″ strips 48–2″ × 20″	34–2″ strips 68–2″ × 20″
Number of strips × width of fabric Number of pieces (I)	17–2″ strips 67–2″ × 9½″	32–2″ strips 127–2″ × 9½″	45–2″ strips 180–2″ × 9½″
Number of strips × width of fabric Number of pieces (G)	4–2″ strips 22–2″ × 6½″	5–2″ strips 30–2″ × 6½″	6–2″ strips 36–2″ × 6½″
Number of strips × width of fabric Number of squares (H)	2–2″ strips 26–2″ × 2″	2–2″ strips 34–2″ × 2″	2–2″ strips 40–2″ × 2″

MAIN LIGHT CUTTING TRADITIONAL FLYING GEESE METHOD

CUT THE STRIPS, AND FROM THOSE STRIPS CUT THE SMALLER PIECES.

	TWIN	FULL / QUEEN	KING
Number of strips × width of fabric Number of pieces (B)	10–2″ strips 112–2″ × 3½″	19–2″ strips 224–2″ × 3½″	27–2″ strips 324–2″ × 3½″
Number of strips × width of fabric Number of pieces	12–2″ strips 24–2″ × 20″	24–2″ strips 48–2″ × 20″	34–2″ strips 68–2″ × 20″
Number of strips × width of fabric Number of pieces (I)	17–2″ strips 67–2″ × 9½″	32–2″ strips 127–2″ × 9½″	45–2″ strips 180–2″ × 9½″
Number of strips × width of fabric Number of pieces (G)	4–2″ strips 22–2″ × 6½″	5–2″ strips 30–2″ × 6½″	6–2″ strips 36–2″ × 6½″
Number of strips × width of fabric Number of squares (H)	2–2″ strips 30–2″ × 2″	2–2″ strips 34–2″ × 2″	2–2″ strips 40–2″ × 2″

You will have extra fat quarter pieces for all sizes of quilts.

Spider

Designed by Monique Dillard
Made and quilted by Sue Glorch

FINISHED BLOCK: 12″ × 12″
FINISHED QUILT: 66″ × 90″, 24 blocks

Information for making alternative quilt sizes is found on page 36.

Materials

- Main light: 2½ yards

- Dark fabric: 12 fat quarters

- First and third borders: 1 yard

- Second border: 1⅝ yards

- Binding: ⅔ yard

- Backing: 5½ yards

- Batting: 76″ × 100″

- Optional: Fit to be Square ruler (page 63)

Cutting Instructions

Work on 1 fat quarter at a time. Each fat quarter, along with the main light, makes 2 blocks.

MAIN LIGHT

Fit to be Square Method (page 7)

- Cut 3 strips 5″ × width of fabric; cut into 24 squares 5″ × 5″, and cut diagonally twice to make 96 triangles (A).

- Cut 10 strips 4″ × width of fabric; cut into 96 squares 4″ × 4″ (D).

- Cut 8 strips 3½″ × width of fabric; cut into 96 squares 3½″ × 3½″ (F).

OR

Traditional Square-in-a-Square Method (page 7)

- Cut 3 strips 4½″ × width of fabric; cut into 24 squares 4½″ × 4½″, and cut diagonally twice to make 96 triangles (A).

- Cut 10 strips 4″ × width of fabric; cut into 96 squares 4″ × 4″ (D).

- Cut 8 strips 3½″ × width of fabric; cut into 96 squares 3½″ × 3½″ (F).

DARK FAT QUARTERS

Fit to be Square Method (page 7)

- From each:

  Cut 1 strip 5″ × width of fabric; cut 2 squares 5″ × 5″ and 2 squares 4¾″ × 4¾″ (C); cut the 5″ × 5″ squares diagonally twice to make 8 triangles (B).

  Cut 2 strips 4″ × width of fabric; cut into 8 squares 4″ × 4″ (E).

OR

Traditional Square-in-a-Square Method (page 7)

- From each:

  Cut 1 strip 4¾″ × width of fabric; cut 2 squares 4½″ × 4½″ and 2 squares 4¾″ × 4¾″ (C); cut the 4½″ × 4½″ squares diagonally twice to make 8 triangles (B).

  Cut 2 strips 4″ × width of fabric; cut into 8 squares 4″ × 4″ (E).

FIRST AND THIRD BORDERS

- Cut 15 strips 2″ × width of fabric.

SECOND BORDER

- Cut 8 strips 6½″ × width of fabric.

BINDING

- Cut 8 strips 2¼″ × width of fabric.

Piecing

1. *Fit to be Square Method (page 7)*

Sew a main light triangle cut from a 5″ × 5″ square (A) to a dark fat quarter triangle cut from a 5″ × 5″ square (B) to make another triangle. Make sure it looks exactly like the diagram, with the main light on the left and the dark on the right. Press toward the dark. Repeat to make 8 per dark fat quarter.

OR

Traditional Square-in-a-Square Method (page 7)

Sew a main light triangle cut from a 4½″ × 4½″ square (A) to a dark fat quarter triangle cut from a 4½″ × 4½″ square (B) to make another triangle. Make sure it looks exactly like the diagram, with the main light on the left and the dark on the right. Press toward the dark. Repeat to make 8 per dark fat quarter.

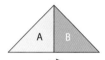

Make 8 from each dark fat quarter.

2. Sew the pieces from Step 1 to opposite sides of the dark 4¾″ × 4¾″ square (C) as shown. Press in the direction of the arrows. Sew 2 more pieces to the other sides. Press in the direction of the arrows. Square to 6½″ × 6½″ using the Fit to be Square ruler or your square ruler. Repeat to make 2 per dark fat quarter.

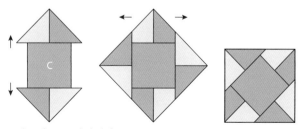

Make 2 from each dark fat quarter.

Note: To match piece C and the triangle from Step 1, finger-press piece C into quarters to find the center of the side and match it to the seam on the triangle.

3. Make 16 half-square triangle units (page 5) from the main light and dark fat quarters using 8 main light 4″ × 4″ squares (D) and 8 dark 4″ × 4″ squares (E). Trim the squares to 3½″ × 3½″.

Make 16.

4. Sew 2 of the pieces from Step 3 together as shown. Watch the placement of the half-square triangles to make sure they look exactly like the diagram. Press in the direction of the arrow. Repeat to make 8.

Make 8.

5. Sew the block together using the pieces from Step 2 and Step 4 and 4 main light 3½″ × 3½″ squares (F). Press in the direction of the arrows. Square the block to 12½″ × 12½″. Repeat to make 2 per dark fat quarter for the total number of blocks needed to complete your desired quilt size. (For the 66″ × 90″ quilt, page 32, make 24 blocks.)

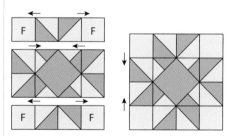

Make 2 from each fat quarter.

Reminder: Watch the placement of half-square triangles. It is really easy to turn them around.

Quilt Construction

Refer to the quilt photo on page 32 and the quilt assembly diagram.

1. Arrange and sew your quilt in rows. Press in the direction of the arrows.

2. Sew on the first border, the second border, and then the third border (see Quiltmaking Basics, page 61). Press toward the borders.

3. Quilt, bind, and enjoy! (See Quiltmaking Basics, page 61.)

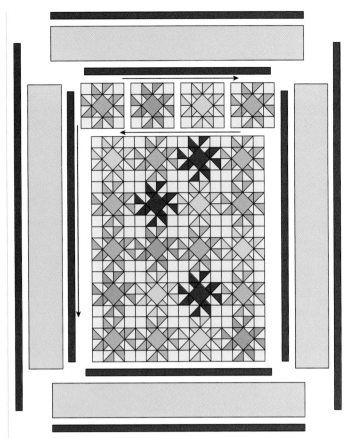

Quilt assembly diagram

ALTERNATIVE QUILT SIZES	FULL / QUEEN	KING
Number of blocks	42	64
Number of blocks, wide × long	6 × 7	8 × 8
Finished size	90″ × 102″	114″ × 114″
YARDAGE		
Main light	4⅜ yards	6⅜ yards
Dark fat quarters	21	32
First and third borders	1¼ yards	1½ yards
Second border	1¾ yards	2 yards
Binding	⅞ yard	1 yard
Backing	8⅓ yards	10⅓ yards
Batting	100″ × 112″	124″ × 124″

MAIN LIGHT CUTTING
FIT TO BE SQUARE METHOD

CUT THE STRIPS, AND FROM THOSE STRIPS CUT THE SMALLER PIECES.

	FULL / QUEEN	KING
Number of strips × width of fabric Number of squares–cut diagonally twice (A) triangles	6–5″ strips 42–5″ × 5″	8–5″ strips 64–5″ × 5″
Number of strips × width of fabric Number of squares (D)	17–4″ strips 168–4″ × 4″	26–4″ strips 256–4″ × 4″
Number of strips × width of fabric Number of squares (F)	14–3½″ strips 168–3½″ × 3½″	22–3½″ strips 256–3½″ × 3½″

MAIN LIGHT CUTTING
TRADITIONAL SQUARE-IN-A-SQUARE METHOD

CUT THE STRIPS, AND FROM THOSE STRIPS CUT THE SMALLER PIECES.

	FULL / QUEEN	KING
Number of strips × width of fabric Number of squares–cut diagonally twice (A) triangles	5–4½″ strips 42–4½″ × 4½″	8–4½″ strips 64–4½″ × 4½″
Number of strips × width of fabric Number of squares (D)	17–4″ strips 168–4″ × 4″	26–4″ strips 256–4″ × 4″
Number of strips × width of fabric Number of squares (F)	14–3½″ strips 168–3½″ × 3½″	22–3½″ strips 256–3½″ × 3½″

Golf

Designed and made by Monique Dillard
Quilted by LeAnne Olson

FINISHED BLOCK: 10½″ × 10½″
FINISHED QUILT: 56″ × 77″, 24 blocks

Information for making alternative quilt sizes is on page 40.

Materials

- Main light fabric: 1½ yards
- Black fabric: 4 fat quarters
- Green fabric: 8 fat quarters
- Inner border: ⅝ yard
- Outer border: 1⅓ yards
- Binding: ⅔ yard
- Backing: 4⅞ yards
- Batting: 66″ × 87″

Cutting Instructions

Before beginning, match 2 greens with 1 black into sets for piecing. Cut the fat quarters separately. Each set of green and half of the black pieces, along with the main light, make 3 blocks.

MAIN LIGHT

- Cut 4 strips 2¾″ × width of fabric; cut into 48 squares 2¾″ × 2¾″ (A).
- Cut 16 strips 2¼″ × width of fabric; cut into 16 pieces 2¼″ × 21″ for strip piecing and 144 squares 2¼″ × 2¼″ (D).

BLACK FAT QUARTERS

- From each:

  Cut 3 strips 4″ × width of fabric; cut into 12 pieces 4″ × 5″ (F).

  Cut 2 strips 2¼″ × width of fabric; cut into 12 squares 2¼″ × 2¼″ (C).

GREEN FAT QUARTERS

- From each:

  Cut 1 strip 2¾″ × width of fabric; cut into 6 squares 2¾″ × 2¾″ (B).

  Cut 2 strips 2¼″ × width of fabric for strip piecing.

  Cut 2 strips 2¼″ × width of fabric; cut into 12 pieces 2¼″ × 3¼″ (E).

INNER BORDER

- Cut 6 strips 1½″ × width of fabric.
- Cut 4 squares 6½″ × 6½″ (G).

OUTER BORDER

- Cut 6 strips 6½″ × width of fabric.

BINDING

- Cut 8 strips 2½″ × width of fabric.

Piecing

1. Make 12 half-square triangle units (page 5) from each green fat quarter and main light using 6 main light 2¾″ × 2¾″ squares (A) and 6 green 2¾″ × 2¾″ squares (B). Trim the squares to 2¼″ × 2¼″.

Make 12 from each green fat quarter.

2. Using 2 half-square triangles from Step 1, a black 2¼″ × 2¼″ square (C), and a main light 2¼″ × 2¼″ square (D), piece a unit as shown. Press in the direction of the arrows. Square to 4″ × 4″. Repeat to make 6 per green fat quarter.

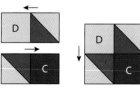

Make 6 from each green fat quarter.

3. Sew a main light 2¼″ × 21″ piece to a green strip 2¼″ × width of fabric. Press toward the green. Repeat to make 2. Cut the strips into 18 pieces 2¼″ wide. Rotate 1 piece and sew together to make a Four-Patch. Make 9 per green fat quarter.

2¼″

Make 9 Four-Patch squares from each green fat quarter.

4. Make 12 combination units (refer to Combination Units, page 5) for each fat quarter, using 12 green 2¼″ × 3¼″ pieces (E), 12 main light 2¼″ × 2¼″ squares (D), and 6 black 4″ × 5″ pieces (F). Press in the direction of the arrows. Square to 4″ × 4″.

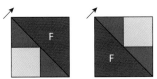

E D

D E

Make 6 from each green fat quarter.

F

F

Make 12.

5. Sew the block together using the units from Steps 2, 3, and 4. Press in the direction of the arrows. Square the block to 11″ × 11″. Make 3 blocks from each green fat quarter. You will have half of the black pieces from each fat quarter left; use them with another green fat quarter.

6. Repeat Steps 1–5 to make the number of blocks needed to complete your desired quilt size. (For the 56″ × 77″ quilt, page 37, make 24 blocks.)

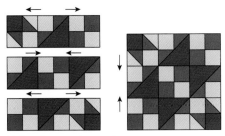

Make 3 from each green fat quarter.

Quilt Construction

Refer to the quilt photo on page 37 and to the quilt assembly diagram.

1. Arrange and sew your quilt in rows. Press in the direction of the arrows.

2. Sew on the inner border and then the outer border, with the inner border fabric 6½″ × 6½″ squares (G) in the corners. (See Quiltmaking Basics, page 61.) Press away from the center.

Quilt assembly diagram

3. Quilt, bind, and enjoy! (See Quiltmaking Basics, page 61.)

ALTERNATIVE QUILT SIZES	TWIN	FULL / QUEEN	KING
Number of blocks	35*	63	81
Number of blocks, wide × long	5 × 7	7 × 9	9 × 9
Finished size	66½″ × 87½″	87½″ × 108½″	108½″ × 108½″
YARDAGE			
Main light	2⅛ yards	3⅝ yards	4¾ yards
Black fat quarters	6	8	14
Green fat quarters	12	16	28
Inner border	⅝ yard	¾ yard	¾ yard
Outer border	1½ yards	2 yards	2¼ yards
Binding	⅔ yard	⅞ yard	1 yard
Backing	5½ yards	8¼ yards	10 yards
Batting	76″ × 97″	97″ × 118″	118″ × 118″
MAIN LIGHT CUTTING	CUT THE STRIPS, AND FROM THOSE STRIPS CUT THE SMALLER PIECES.		
Number of strips × width of fabric Number of squares (A)	5–2¾″ strips 70–2¾″ × 2¾″	9–2¾″ strips 126–2¾″ × 2¾″	12–2¾″ strips 162–2¾″ × 2¾″
Number of strips × width of fabric Number of pieces	12–2¼″ strips 24–2¼″ × 21″	21–2¼″ strips 42–2¼″ × 21″	27–2¼″ strips 54–2¼″ × 21″
Number of strips × width of fabric Number of squares (D)	13–2¼″ strips 210–2¼″ × 2¼″	23–2¼″ strips 378–2¼″ × 2¼″	29–2¼″ strips 486–2¼″ × 2¼″

You will have extra fat quarter pieces.

Memory

Designed by Monique Dillard
Made by Peggy Drake
Quilted by LeAnne Olson

FINISHED BLOCK: 8¾″ × 8¾″
FINISHED QUILT: 67″ × 84½″, 48 blocks

Information for making alternative quilt sizes is on page 44.

Materials

- Main light fabric: 2½ yards

- Pink and red fabrics: 8 fat quarters total

- Brown fabric: 8 fat quarters

- First border: ½ yard

- Second border: ⅜ yard

- Third border: 1¼ yards

- Binding: ⅔ yard

- Backing: 5⅓ yards

- Batting: 77″ × 94″

Cutting Instructions

Before beginning, match your pink and brown fat quarters into pairs for piecing. Cut the fat quarters with right sides together. Each set of pink/red and brown fat quarters, along with the main light, makes 6 blocks: 3 pink/red blocks and 3 brown blocks.

MAIN LIGHT

- Cut 20 strips 2¼″ × width of fabric; cut into 192 pieces 2¼″ × 4″ (D).

- Cut 14 strips 2¾″ × width of fabric; cut into 192 squares 2¾″ × 2¾″ (A).

PINK / RED FAT QUARTERS

- From each:

  Cut 3 strips 2¼″ × width of fabric; cut into 27 squares 2¼″ × 2¼″ (E).

  Cut 2 strips 2¾″ × width of fabric; cut into 12 squares 2¾″ × 2¾″ (B).

BROWN FAT QUARTERS

- From each:

  Cut 3 strips 2¼″ × width of fabric; cut into 27 squares 2¼″ × 2¼″ (C).

  Cut 2 strips 2¾″ × width of fabric; cut into 12 squares 2¾″ × 2¾″ (F).

FIRST BORDER

- Cut 7 strips 2¼″ × width of fabric.

SECOND BORDER

- Cut 7 strips 1½″ × width of fabric.

THIRD BORDER

- Cut 8 strips 5″ × width of fabric.

BINDING

- Cut 8 strips 2½″ × width of fabric.

Piecing

1. Make 24 half-square triangles (page 5) using 12 main light 2¾″ × 2¾″ (A) squares and 12 pink/red 2¾″ × 2¾″ (B) squares. Trim the squares to 2¼″ × 2¼″.

Make 24.

2. Sew the center of the pink/red half-square triangle block together using 4 of the half-square triangles from Step 1 and 5 brown 2¼″ × 2¼″ squares (C). Press in the direction of the arrows. Square the block to 5¾″ × 5¾″. Repeat to make 3 blocks with the pink/red half-square triangles.

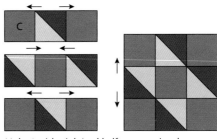

Make 3 with pink/red half-square triangles.

3. Sew a half-square triangle from Step 1 to the end of a main light 2¼″ × 4″ piece (D). Watch the placement of the half-square triangle. Press in the direction of the arrow. Repeat to make 6 per pink / red half-square triangle. Sew another half-square triangle from Step 1 to the other end of a main light 2¼″ × 4″ piece (D). Watch the placement of the half-square triangle. Press in the direction of the arrow. Repeat to make 6 of each using pink / red half-square triangles.

Make 6 of each with pink / red half-square triangles.

4. Sew the pink / red half-square triangle block together using the pieces from Steps 2 and 3, along with 4 pink / red 2¼″ × 2¼″ squares (E). Square the block to 9¼″ × 9¼″. Repeat to make 3 blocks with the pink / red half-square triangles from each fat quarter combination for your desired quilt size. (For the 67″ × 84½″ quilt, page 41, make 24 pink / red blocks.)

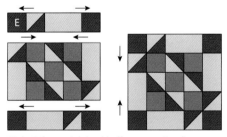

Make 3 from pink / red half-square triangles.

5. Make 24 half-square triangles (page 5) using 12 main light 2¾″ × 2¾″ (A) squares and 12 brown 2¾″ × 2¾″ (F) squares. Trim the squares to 2¼″ × 2¼″.

Make 24 from each pair of main light and brown.

6. Sew the center of the brown half-square triangle block together using 4 of the half-square triangles from Step 5 and 5 pink / red 2¼″ × 2¼″ squares (E). Press in the direction of the arrows. Square the block to 5¾″ × 5¾″. Repeat to make 3 blocks with the brown half-square triangles.

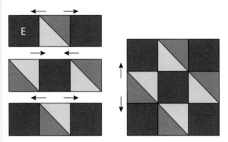

Make 3 with brown half-square triangles.

7. Sew a half-square triangle from Step 5 to the end of a main light 2¼″ × 4″ piece (D). Watch the placement of the half-square triangle. Press in the direction of the arrow. Repeat to make 6 per brown half-square triangle. Sew another half-square triangle from Step 5 to the other end of a main light 2¼″ × 4″ piece (D). Watch the placement of the half-square triangle. Press in the direction of the arrow. Repeat to make 6 of each using brown half-square triangles.

Make 6 of each with brown half-square triangles.

8. Sew the brown block together using the pieces from Steps 6 and 7, along with 4 brown 2¼″ × 2¼″ squares (C). Square the block to 9¼″ × 9¼″. Repeat to make 3 blocks with the brown half-square triangles from each fat quarter combination to complete your desired quilt size. (For the 67″ × 84½″ quilt, page 41, make 24 brown blocks.)

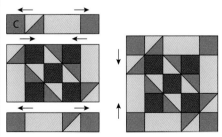

Make 3 from brown half-square triangles.

Quilt Construction

Refer to the quilt photo on page 41 and the quilt assembly diagram.

1. Arrange and sew your quilt in rows. Press in the direction of the arrows.

2. Sew on the inner border and then the outer border. (See Quiltmaking Basics, page 61.) Press toward the borders.

3. Quilt, bind, and enjoy! (See Quiltmaking Basics, page 61.)

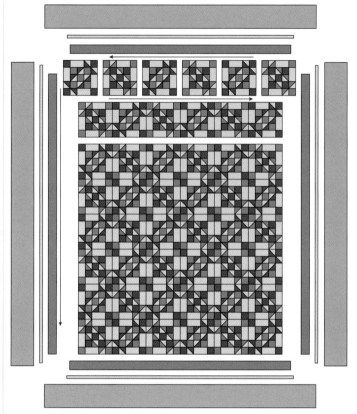

Quilt assembly diagram

ALTERNATIVE QUILT SIZES	TWIN	FULL / QUEEN	KING
Number of blocks	54	90	121*
Number of blocks, wide by long	6 × 9	9 × 10	11 × 11
Finished size	67″ × 93¼″	93¼″ × 102″	110¾″ × 110¾″
YARDAGE			
Main light	2⅞ yards	4½ yards	6 yards
Brown fat quarters	9	15	21
Pink fat quarters	9	15	21
First border	⅝ yard	¾ yard	⅞ yard
Second border	½ yard	⅝ yard	⅝ yard
Third border	1½ yards	1⅔ yards	2 yards
Binding	¾ yard	⅞ yard	1 yard
Backing	5¾ yards	8⅔ yards	10¼ yards
Batting	77″ × 104″	104″ × 112″	122″ × 122″
MAIN LIGHT CUTTING	CUT THE STRIPS, AND FROM THOSE STRIPS CUT THE SMALLER PIECES.		
Number of strips × width of fabric Number of pieces (E)	22–2¼″ strips 216–2¼″ × 4″	36–2¼″ strips 360–2¼″ × 4″	49–2¼″ strips 484–2¼″ × 4″
Number of strips × width of fabric Number of squares (A)	16–2¾″ strips 216–2¾″ × 2¾″	26–2¾″ strips 360–2¾″ × 2¾″	35–2¾″ strips 484–2¾″ × 2¾″

* You will have extra fat quarter pieces for the king-size quilt.

Baccarat

Designed and made by Monique Dillard
Quilted by LeAnne Olson

FINISHED BLOCK: 16″ × 16″
FINISHED QUILT: 60″ × 76″, 12 blocks

Information for making alternative quilt sizes is on page 49.

Materials

- Main light fabric: 3½ yards

- Dark fabric: 12 fat quarters

- Outer border: 1⅝ yards

- Binding: ⅔ yard

- Backing: 4¾ yards

- Batting: 70″ × 86″

- Optional: Fit to be Geese ruler (page 63)

Cutting Instructions

Each fat quarter, along with the main light, is enough to make 1 block.

MAIN LIGHT
Fit to be Geese Method (page 6)

- Cut 8 strips 6½″ × width of fabric; cut into 48 squares 6½″ × 6½″ (H).

- Cut 2 strips 5½″ × width of fabric; cut into 12 squares 5½″ × 5½″, and cut diagonally twice to make 48 triangles (B).

- Cut 2 strips 4½″ × width of fabric; cut into 12 squares 4½″ × 4½″ (I).

- Cut 4 strips 3″ × width of fabric; cut into 48 squares 3″ × 3″ (C).

- Cut 12 strips 2½″ × width of fabric; cut into 192 squares 2½″ × 2½″ (E).

OR

Traditional Flying Geese Method (page 6)

- Cut 8 strips 6½″ × width of fabric; cut into 48 squares 6½″ × 6½″ (H).

- Cut 3 strips 4½″ × width of fabric; cut into 48 pieces 4½″ × 2½″ (B).

- Cut 2 strips 4½″ × width of fabric; cut into 12 squares 4½″ × 4½″ (I).

- Cut 4 strips 3″ × width of fabric; cut into 48 squares 3″ × 3″ (C).

- Cut 12 strips 2½″ × width of fabric; cut into 192 squares 2½″ × 2½″ (E).

DARK FAT QUARTERS
Fit to be Geese Method (page 6)

- From each dark fat quarter:

  Cut 1 strip 3¼″ × width of fabric; cut into 4 squares 3¼″ × 3¼″, and cut diagonally once to make 8 triangles (A).

  Cut 1 strip 3″ × width of fabric; cut into 4 squares 3″ × 3″ (D).

  Cut 4 strips 2½″ × width of fabric; cut into 8 pieces 2½″ × 4½″ (G) and 16 squares 2½″ × 2½″ (F).

OR

Traditional Flying Geese Method (page 6)

- From each dark fat quarter:

  Cut 1 strip 3″ × width of fabric; cut into 4 squares 3″ × 3″ (D).

  Cut 6 strips 2½″ × width of fabric; cut into 8 pieces 2½″ × 4½″ (G) and 32 squares 2½″ × 2½″ (A and F).

BORDER
- Cut 8 strips 6½″ × width of fabric.

BINDING
- Cut 8 strips 2½″ × width of fabric.

Piecing

1. Make 48 Flying Geese units measuring 2½″ × 4½″ for the main light and various dark fat quarters.

For the Fit to be Geese Method (page 6), use 96 dark triangles cut from 3¼″ × 3¼″ squares cut diagonally once (A) and 48 main light triangles cut from 5½″ × 5½″ squares cut diagonally twice (B).

OR

For the Traditional Flying Geese Method (page 6), use 96 dark 2½″ × 2½″ squares (A) and 48 main light 2½″ × 4½″ pieces (B).

Make 48.

2. Make 96 half-square triangle units (page 5) from the main light and dark fat quarters using 48 main light 3″ × 3″ squares (C) and 48 dark 3″ × 3″ squares (D). Trim the squares to 2½″ × 2½″.

Make 96.

3. Sew the half-square triangle units from Step 2 and 96 main light 2½″ × 2½″ squares (E) together as shown. Press in the direction of the arrows. Square to 4½″ × 4½″. Repeat to make 48.

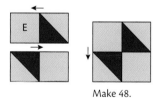

Make 48.

4. Sew the units from Step 3 to the Flying Geese from Step 1 as shown. Press in the direction of the arrow. Repeat to make 48.

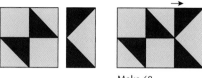

Make 48.

5. Sew a main light 2½″ × 2½″ square (E) to a dark 2½″ × 2½″ square (F). Press toward the dark. Repeat to make 96. Sew a dark 2½″ × 4½″ piece (G) to the piece you just made. Press toward the dark. Repeat to make 96.

Make 96.

6. On the backs of the pieces from Step 5, draw a diagonal line from corner to corner as shown. Place a drawn piece on a main light 6½″ × 6½″ square (H) right sides together as shown. Watch the placement of the light square. Sew directly on the line and press in the direction of the arrow. Trim the bottom layers to ¼″. Place another drawn piece right sides together on the opposite corner. Sew directly on the line and press in the direction of the arrow. Trim the bottom layers to ¼″. On the backs of 48 dark 2½″ × 2½″ squares (F), draw a diagonal line from corner to corner. Place the drawn square on the corner of the piece you just made as shown. Sew directly on the line and press in the direction of the arrow. Trim the bottom layers to ¼″. Square to 6½″ × 6½″. Repeat to make 48.

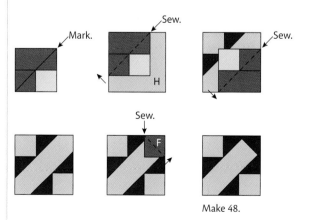

Make 48.

7. On the backs of 48 dark 2½″ × 2½″ squares (F), draw a diagonal line from corner to corner. Place a drawn square on a main light 4½″ × 4½″ square (I) with right sides together. Sew exactly on the line and press in the direction of the arrow. Trim the bottom layers to ¼″. Sew another dark 2½″ × 2½″ square (F) on the opposite corner. Press in the direction of the arrow. Place 2 more drawn dark 2½″ × 2½″ squares (F) on the opposite corners of the piece you just made. Sew directly on the lines and press in the direction of the arrows. Trim the bottom layers to ¼″. Square to 4½″ × 4½″. Make 12.

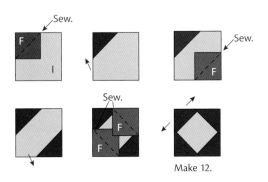

Make 12.

8. Sew the block together using the pieces from Step 4, Step 6, and Step 7. Press in the direction of the arrows. Square the block to 16½″ × 16½″. Repeat to make the number of blocks needed to complete your desired quilt size. (For the 60″ × 76″ quilt, page 45, make 12 blocks.)

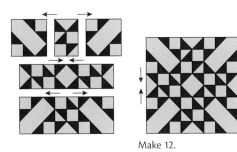

Make 12.

Quilt Construction

Refer to the quilt photo on page 45 and the quilt assembly diagram.

1. Arrange and sew your quilt in rows. Press in the direction of the arrows.

2. Sew on the border (see Quiltmaking Basics, page 61). Press toward the borders.

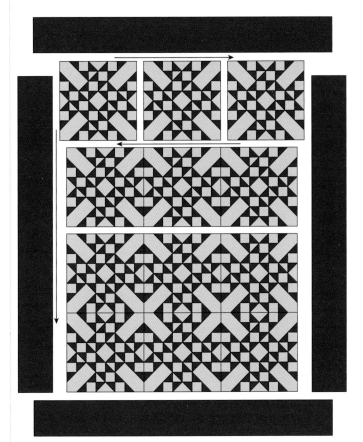

Quilt assembly diagram

3. Quilt, bind, and enjoy! (See Quiltmaking Basics, page 61.)

ALTERNATIVE QUILT SIZES	TWIN	FULL / QUEEN	KING
Number of blocks	15	30	36
Number of blocks, wide × long	3 × 5	5 × 6	6 × 6
Finished size	60″ × 92″	92″ × 108″	108″ × 108″
YARDAGE			
Main light	4¼ yards	8¼ yards	9¾ yards
Dark fat quarters	15	30	36
Border	1⅝ yards	2 yards	2¼ yards
Binding	¾ yard	⅞ yard	1 yard
Backing	5⅔ yards	8½ yards	10 yards
Batting	70″ × 102″	102″ × 118″	118″ × 118″
MAIN LIGHT CUTTING FIT TO BE GEESE METHOD	CUT THE STRIPS, AND FROM THOSE STRIPS CUT THE SMALLER PIECES.		
Number of strips × width of fabric Number of squares (H)	10–6½″ strips 60–6½″ × 6½″	20–6½″ strips 120–6½″ × 6½″	24–6½″ strips 144–6½″ × 6½″
Number of strips × width of fabric Number of squares–cut diagonally twice (B) triangles	3–5½″ strips 15–5½″ × 5½″	5–5½″ strips 30–5½″ × 5½″	6–5½″ strips 36–5½″ × 5½″
Number of strips × width of fabric Number of squares (I)	2–4½″ strips 15–4½″ × 4½″	4–4½″ strips 30–4½″ × 4½″	4–4½″ strips 36–4½″ × 4½″
Number of strips × width of fabric Number of squares (C)	5–3″ strips 60–3″ × 3″	10–3″ strips 120–3″ × 3″	12–3″ strips 144–3″ × 3″
Number of strips × width of fabric Number of squares (E)	15–2½″ strips 240–2½″ × 2½″	30–2½″ strips 480–2½″ × 2½″	36–2½″ strips 576–2½″ × 2½″
MAIN LIGHT CUTTING TRADITIONAL FLYING GEESE METHOD	CUT THE STRIPS, AND FROM THOSE STRIPS CUT THE SMALLER PIECES.		
Number of strips × width of fabric Number of squares (H)	10–6½″ strips 60–6½″ × 6½″	20–6½″ strips 120–6½″ × 6½″	24–6½″ strips 144–6½″ × 6½″
Number of strips × width of fabric Number of pieces (B)	4–4½″ strips 60–4½″ × 2½″	8–4½″ strips 120–4½″ × 2½″	9–4½″ strips 144–4½″ × 2½″
Number of strips × width of fabric Number of squares (I)	2–4½″ strips 15–4½″ × 4½″	4–4½″ strips 30–4½″ × 4½″	4–4½″ strips 36–4½″ × 4½″
Number of strips × width of fabric Number of squares (C)	5–3″ strips 60–3″ × 3″	10–3″ strips 120–3″ × 3″	12–3″ strips 144–3″ × 3″
Number of strips × width of fabric Number of squares (E)	15–2½″ strips 240–2½″ × 2½″	30–2½″ strips 480–2½″ × 2½″	36–2½″ strips 576–2½″ × 2½″

Freecell

Designed and made by Monique Dillard
Quilted by Danette Gonzalez

FINISHED BLOCK: 10½″ × 10½″
FINISHED QUILT: 56″ × 67″, 24 blocks

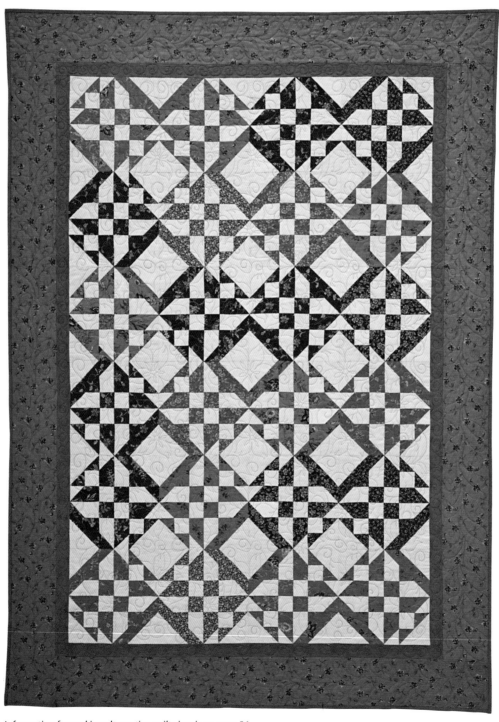

Information for making alternative quilt sizes is on page 54.

Materials

- Main light fabric: 2⅓ yards

- Dark fabric: 12 fat quarters

- Inner border: ⅓ yard

- Outer border: 1½ yards

- Binding: ⅔ yard

- Backing: 3⅔ yards

- Batting: 66″ × 77″

- Optional: Fit to be Quarter ruler (page 63)

Cutting Instructions

Work on 1 fat quarter at a time. Each fat quarter, along with the main light, makes 2 blocks.

MAIN LIGHT

- Cut 21 strips 2¼″ × width of fabric; cut into 12 pieces 2¼″ × 10″, 144 squares 2¼″ × 2¼″ (C), and 96 pieces 2¼″ × 4″ (H).

- Cut 3 strips 4½″ × width of fabric; cut into 24 squares 4½″ × 4½″ (B).

- Cut 3 strips 5″ × width of fabric; cut into 24 pieces 5″ × 4″ (F).

DARK FAT QUARTERS

- From each:

  Cut 1 strip 4½″ × width of fabric; cut into 2 squares 4½″ × 4½″ (A) and 4 pieces 2¼″ × 3¼″ (D).

Cut 4 strips 2¼″ × width of fabric; cut into 1 piece 2¼″ × 10″, 8 pieces 2¼″ × 4″ (J), and 8 squares 2¼″ × 2¼″ (G).

INNER BORDER

- Cut 6 strips 1½″ × width of fabric.

OUTER BORDER

- Cut 7 strips 6½″ × width of fabric.

BINDING

- Cut 7 strips 2½″ × width of fabric.

Piecing

1. Make 4 half-square triangle units (page 5) from each dark fat quarter and main light using 2 dark fat quarter 4½″ × 4½″ squares (A) and 2 main light 4½″ × 4½″ squares (B). Trim the squares to 4″ × 4″.

Make 4 half-square triangles from each.

2. Make 4 combination units (refer to Combination Units, page 5) for each fat quarter using 4 dark 2¼″ × 3¼″ pieces (D), 4 main light 2¼″ × 2¼″ squares (C), and 2 main light 4″ × 5″ pieces (F). Press in the direction of the arrows. Trim squares to 4″ × 4″.

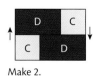

Make 2.

Make 4.

3. On the backs of 4 dark 2¼″ × 2¼″ squares (G), draw a diagonal line from corner to corner. Place a drawn dark square on a main light 2¼″ × 4″ piece (H) right sides together. Sew directly on the line and press toward the dark. Trim the bottom 2 layers to ¼″. Watch the angle of the stitching line, and make sure that the piece looks exactly as shown. Make 4 for each dark fat quarter.

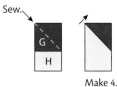

Make 4.

4. On the backs of 4 main light 2¼" × 2¼" squares (C), draw a diagonal line from corner to corner. Place a drawn main light square on a dark 2¼" × 4" piece (J) right sides together. Sew directly on the line, and press toward the dark. Trim the bottom 2 layers to ¼". Watch the angle of the stitching line, and make sure that the piece looks exactly as shown. Make 4 for each dark fat quarter.

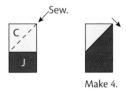

Make 4.

5. Sew the pieces from Steps 3 and 4 together as shown. Press in the direction of the arrows. Square to 4" × 4". Repeat to make 4.

Make 4.

6. On the backs of 4 dark 2¼" × 2¼" squares (G), draw a diagonal line from corner to corner. Place a drawn dark square on a main light 2¼" × 4" piece (H) right sides together. Sew directly on the line, and press toward the dark. Trim the bottom 2 layers to ¼". Watch the angle of the stitching line, and make sure that the piece looks exactly as shown, which is mirrors Step 3. Make 4 for each dark fat quarter.

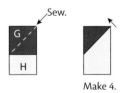

Make 4.

7. On the backs of 4 main light 2¼" × 2¼" squares (C), draw a diagonal line from corner to corner. Place a drawn main light square on a dark 2¼" × 4" piece (J) right sides together. Sew directly on the line and press toward the dark. Trim the bottom 2 layers to ¼". Watch the angle of the stitching line, and make sure that the piece looks

exactly as shown, which mirrors Step 5. Make 4 for each dark fat quarter.

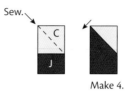

Make 4.

8. Sew the pieces from Steps 6 and 7 together as shown. Press in the direction of the arrows. Square to 4" × 4". Repeat to make 4.

Make 4.

9. Sew a main light 2¼" × 10" piece to a dark 2¼" × 10" piece. Press toward the dark piece. Cut into 4 segments 2¼" wide. Rotate 1 piece and sew together to make a Four-Patch. Press in one direction. Square to 4" × 4". Repeat to make 2.

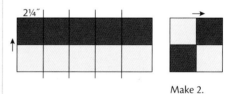

Make 2.

10. Sew the block together using the pieces from Steps 1, 2, 5, 8, and 9. Press the block in the direction of the arrows. Square the block to 11" × 11". Repeat to make 2 per dark fat quarter for the total number of blocks needed to complete your desired quilt size. (For the 56" × 67" quilt, page 50, make 24 blocks.)

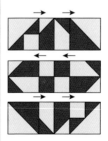
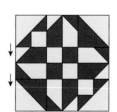

Make 2 per dark fat quarter.

Quilt Construction

Refer to the quilt photo on page 50 and the quilt assembly diagram.

1. Arrange and sew the quilt together in rows. Press in the direction of the arrows.

2. Sew on the inner and the outer borders (see Quiltmaking Basics, page 61). Press toward the borders.

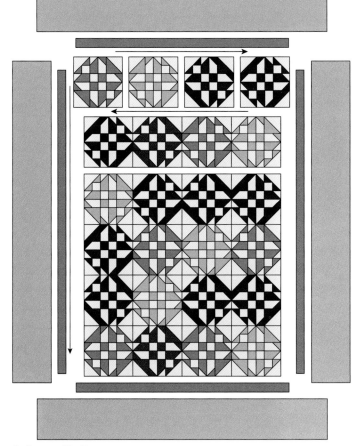

Quilt assembly diagram

3. Quilt, bind, and enjoy! (See Quiltmaking Basics, page 61.)

ALTERNATIVE QUILT SIZES	TWIN	FULL / QUEEN	KING
Number of blocks	35*	63*	64*
Number of blocks, wide × long	5 × 7	7 × 9	9 × 9
Finished size	66½" × 87½"	87½" × 108½"	108½" × 108½"
YARDAGE			
Main light	3⅜ yards	5⅞ yards	7⅜ yards
Dark fat quarters	18	32	41
Inner border	½ yard	½ yard	⅔ yard
Outer border	1½ yards	2⅛ yards	2¼ yards
Binding	¾ yard	¾ yard	1 yard
Backing	5½ yards	8⅓ yards	10⅓ yards
Batting	77" × 98"	98" × 119"	119" × 119"

MAIN LIGHT CUTTING	CUT THE STRIPS, AND FROM THOSE STRIPS CUT THE SMALLER PIECES.		
Number of strips × width of fabric Number of squares (C)	12–2¼" strips 210–2¼" × 2¼"	21–2¼" strips 378–2¼" × 2¼"	27–2¼" strips 486–2¼" × 2¼"
Number of strips × width of fabric Number of pieces	5–2¼" strips 18–2¼" × 10"	8–2¼" strips 32–2¼" × 10"	11–2¼" strips 41–2¼" × 10"
Number of strips × width of fabric Number of pieces (H)	14–2¼" strips 140–2¼" × 4"	26–2¼" strips 252–2¼" × 4"	33–2¼" strips 324–2¼" × 4"
Number of strips × width of fabric Number of squares (B)	4–4½" strips 35–4½" × 4½"	8–4½" strips 63–4½" × 4½"	10–4½" strips 81–4½" × 4½"
Number of strips × width of fabric Number of pieces (F)	4–5" strips 35–5" × 4"	7–5" strips 63–5" × 4"	9–5" strips 81–5" × 4"

You will have extra fat quarter pieces.

Poker

Designed by Monique Dillard
Made by Kathy Rosecrance
Quilted by LeAnne Olson

FINISHED BLOCK: 9″ × 9″
FINISHED QUILT: 59½″ × 77½″, 35 blocks

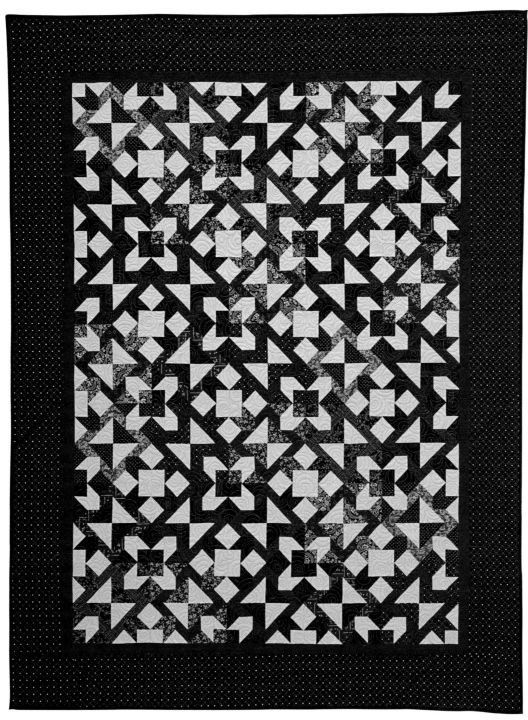

Information for making alternative quilt sizes is on page 60.

Materials

- Main light fabric: 2 yards
- Red fabric: 9 fat quarters
- Black fabric: 9 fat quarters
- Inner border: ½ yard
- Outer border: 1½ yards
- Binding: ⅔ yard
- Backing: 5 yards
- Batting: 70" × 88"
- Optional: Fit to be Geese and Fit to be Quarter rulers (page 63)

Cutting Instructions

Before beginning, match red and black fat quarters into pairs for piecing. Cut the red and black fat quarters separately. Each pair of fat quarters, along with the main light, makes 4 blocks.

MAIN LIGHT
Fit to be Geese Method (page 6)

- Cut 4 strips 4½" × width of fabric; cut into 36 squares 4½" × 4½", and cut diagonally twice to make 144 triangles (A).
- Cut 4 strips 3½" × width of fabric; cut into 36 pieces 3½" × 4½" (F).
- Cut 5 strips 2¾" × width of fabric; cut into 72 squares 2¾" × 2¾", and cut diagonally once to make 144 triangles (I).

- Cut 7 strips 2" × width of fabric; cut into 144 squares 2" × 2" (H).

OR

Traditional Flying Geese Method (page 6)

- Cut 4 strips 3½" × width of fabric; cut into 36 pieces 3½" × 4½" (F).
- Cut 27 strips 2" × width of fabric; cut into 288 squares 2" × 2" (H and I) and 144 pieces 2" × 3½" (A).

RED FAT QUARTERS
Fit to be Geese Method (page 6)

- From each:

  Cut 2 strips 3" × width of fabric; cut into 16 pieces 3" × 2" (E).

  Cut 3 strips 2¾" × width of fabric; cut into 16 squares 2¾" × 2¾", and cut diagonally once to make 32 triangles (B).

OR

Traditional Flying Geese Method (page 6)

- From each:

  Cut 2 strips 3" × width of fabric; cut into 16 pieces 3" × 2" (E).

  Cut 4 strips 2" × width of fabric; cut into 32 squares 2" × 2" (B).

BLACK FAT QUARTERS
Fit to be Geese Method (page 6)

- From each:

  Cut 1 strip 4½" × width of fabric; cut into 4 squares 4½" × 4½", and cut diagonally twice to make 16 triangles (G).

  Cut 1 strip 3½" × width of fabric; cut into 4 pieces 3½" × 4½" (J).

  Cut 2 strips 2¾" × width of fabric; cut into 8 squares 2¾" × 2¾", and cut diagonally once to make 16 triangles (C).

  Cut 2 strips 2" × width of fabric; cut into 16 squares 2" × 2" (D).

OR

Traditional Flying Geese Method (page 6)

- From each:

  Cut 1 strip 3½" × width of fabric; cut into 4 pieces 3½" × 4½" (J).

  Cut 5 strips 2" × width of fabric; cut into 32 squares 2" × 2" (C and D) and 16 pieces 2" × 3½" (G).

INNER BORDER
- Cut 6 strips 1¾" × width of fabric.

OUTER BORDER
- Cut 7 strips 6½" × width of fabric.

BINDING
- Cut 8 strips 2½" × width of fabric.

Piecing

1. Make 8 Flying Geese units measuring 2″ × 3½″ using the main light, red, and black as shown.

For the Fit to be Geese Method (page 6), use 8 red triangles cut from 2¾″ × 2¾″ squares cut diagonally once (B), 8 black triangles cut from 2¾″ × 2¾″ squares cut diagonally once (C), and 8 main light triangles cut from 4½″ × 4½″ squares cut diagonally twice (A). Watch the placement to match the red and black triangles as shown.

OR

For the Traditional Flying Geese Method (page 6), use 8 red 2″ × 2″ squares (B), 8 black 2″ × 2″ squares (C), and 8 main light 2″ × 3½″ squares (A). Watch the placement to match the red and black as shown.

Make 8.

2. Make 8 Flying Geese units measuring 2″ × 3½″ using the main light, red, and black as shown.

For the Fit to be Geese Method (page 6), use 8 red triangles cut from 2¾″ × 2¾″ squares cut diagonally once (B), 8 black triangles cut from 2¾″ × 2¾″ squares cut diagonally once (C), and 8 main light triangles cut from 4½″ × 4½″ squares cut diagonally twice (A). Watch the placement of the red and black triangles as shown below.

OR

For the Traditional Flying Geese Method (page 6), use 8 red 2″ × 2″ squares (B), 8 black 2″ × 2″ squares (C), and 8 main light 2″ × 3½″ pieces (A). Watch the placement to match the red and black as shown.

Make 8.

3. Make 8 combination units (refer to Combination Units, page 5) for each fat quarter using 8 red 2″ × 3″ pieces (E), 8 black 2″ × 2″ squares (D), and 4 main light 3½″ × 4½″ pieces (F). Press in the direction of the arrows. Square to 3½″ × 3½″.

Make 4.

Make 8.

4. Sew a quarter block to the main light background using the pieces from Steps 1, 2, and 3 plus a main light 2″ × 2″ square (H). Press in the direction of the arrows. Square the quarter block to 5″ × 5″. Repeat to make 8 per red and black color pair.

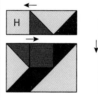

Make 8.

5. Make 8 Flying Geese units measuring 2″ × 3½″ using a black, red, and main light as shown.

For the Fit to be Geese Method (page 6), use 8 red triangles cut from 2¾″ × 2¾″ squares cut diagonally once (B), 8 main light triangles cut from 2¾″ × 2¾″ squares cut diagonally once (I), and 8 black triangles cut from 4½″ × 4½″ squares cut diagonally twice (G). Watch the placement to match the red and main light triangles as shown on page 58.

For the Traditional Flying Geese Method (page 6), use 8 red 2″ × 2″ squares (B), 8 main light 2″ × 2″ squares (I), and 8 black 2″ × 3½″ pieces (G). Watch the placement to match the red and main light as shown.

Make 8.

6. Make 8 Flying Geese units measuring 2″ × 3½″ using the main light, red, and black as shown.

For the Fit to be Geese Method (page 6), use 8 red triangles cut from 2¾″ × 2¾″ squares cut diagonally once (B), 8 main light triangles cut from 2¾″ × 2¾″ squares cut diagonally once (I), and 8 black triangles cut from 4½″ × 4½″ squares cut diagonally twice (G). Watch the placement to match the red and black triangles as shown.

OR

For the Traditional Flying Geese Method (page 6), use 8 red 2″ × 2″ squares (B), 8 main light 2″ × 2″ squares (I), and 8 black 2″ × 3½″ pieces (G). Watch the placement to match the red and main light as shown.

Make 8.

7. Make 4 combination units (refer to Combination Units, page 5) for each fat quarter using 8 red 2″ × 3″ pieces (E), 8 main light 2″ × 2″ squares (H), and 4 black 3½″ × 4½″ pieces (J). Press in the direction of the arrows. Square to 3½″ × 3½″.

Make 4.

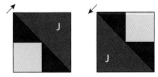

Make 8.

8. Sew a quarter block together with the black background using the pieces from Steps 5, 6, and 7 plus a black 2″ × 2″ square (D). Press in the direction of the arrows. Square the quarter block to 5″ × 5″. Repeat to make 8 per red and black color pair.

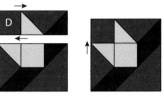

Make 8.

9. Sew the block together in rows using the quarter blocks from Steps 4 and 8. Press in the direction of the arrows. Square the block to 9½″ × 9½″. Repeat to make 4 blocks per red, black, and main light color combination for the total number of blocks needed to complete your desired quilt size. (For the 59½″ × 77½″ quilt, page 55, make 35 blocks. You will have an extra block left over.)

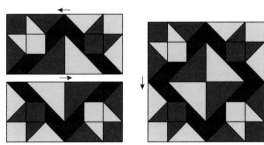

Make 4 for each red and black pair.

Quilt Construction

Refer to the quilt photo on page 55 and the quilt assembly diagram.

1. Arrange and sew your quilt in rows. Press in the direction of the arrows.

2. Sew on the inner and outer borders. (See Quiltmaking Basics, page 61.) Press toward the borders.

Quilt assembly diagram

3. Quilt, bind, and enjoy! (See Quiltmaking Basics, page 61.)

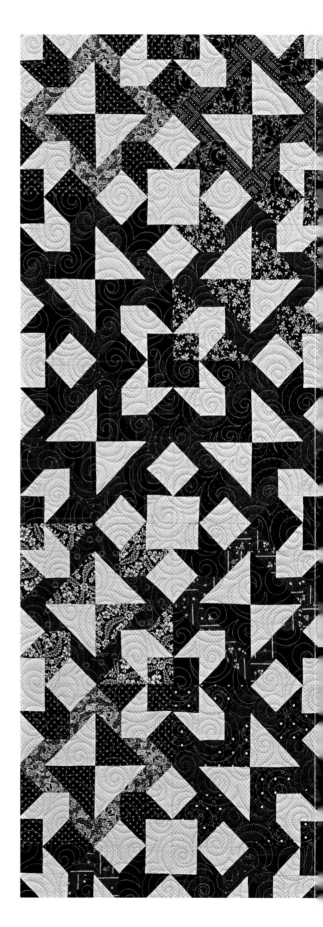

ALTERNATIVE QUILT SIZES	TWIN	FULL / QUEEN	KING
Number of blocks	40	80	121*
Number of blocks, wide × long	5 × 8	8 × 10	11 × 11
Finished size	59½″ × 86½″	86½″ × 104½″	113½″ × 113½″
YARDAGE			
Main light	2⅜ yards	4¼ yards	6¼ yards
Red fat quarters	10	20	31
Black fat quarters	10	20	31
Inner border	½ yard	⅝ yard	¾ yard
Outer border	1⅝ yards	2 yards	2½ yards
Binding	⅔ yard	⅞ yard	1 yard
Backing	5½ yards	8⅛ yards	10 yards
Batting	70″ × 97″	97″ × 115″	123″ × 123″

MAIN LIGHT CUTTING FIT TO BE GEESE METHOD

CUT THE STRIPS, AND FROM THOSE STRIPS CUT THE SMALLER PIECES.

	TWIN	FULL / QUEEN	KING
Number of strips × width of fabric Number of squares–cut diagonally twice (A) triangles	5–4½″ strips 40–4½″ × 4½″	9–4½″ strips 80–4½″ × 4½″	14–4½″ strips 121–4½″ × 4½″
Number of strips × width of fabric Number of pieces (F)	5–3½″ strips 40–3½″ × 4½″	9–3½″ strips 80–3½″ × 4½″	14–3½″ strips 121–3½″ × 4½″
Number of strips × width of fabric Number of squares–cut diagonally once (I) triangles	6–2¾″ strips 80–2¾″ × 2¾″	11–2¾″ strips 160–2¾″ × 2¾″	17–2¾″ strips 242–2¾″ × 2¾″
Number of strips × width of fabric Number of squares (H)	8–2″ strips 160–2″ × 2″	16–2″ strips 320–2″ × 2″	24–2″ strips 484–2″ × 2″

MAIN LIGHT CUTTING TRADITIONAL FLYING GEESE METHOD

CUT THE STRIPS, AND FROM THOSE STRIPS CUT THE SMALLER PIECES.

	TWIN	FULL / QUEEN	KING
Number of strips × width of fabric Number of pieces (A)	5–3½″ strips 40–3½″ × 4½″	9–3½″ strips 80–3½″ × 4½″	14–3½″ strips 121–3½″ × 4½″
Number of strips × width of fabric Number of pieces (F)	5–3½″ strips 40–3½″ × 4½″	9–3½″ strips 80–3½″ × 4½″	14–3½″ strips 121–3½″ × 4½″
Number of strips × width of fabric Number of squares (I)	8–2″ strips 160–2″ × 2″	16–2″ strips 320–2″ × 2″	24–2″ strips 484–2″ × 2″
Number of strips × width of fabric Number of squares (H)	8–2″ strips 160–2″ × 2″	16–2″ strips 320–2″ × 2″	24–2″ strips 484–2″ × 2″

* You will have extra fat quarter pieces.

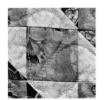

Quiltmaking Basics: How to Finish Your Quilt

General Guidelines

Seam Allowances

A ¼" seam allowance is used for most projects. It's a good idea to do a test seam before you begin sewing to check that your ¼" is accurate. Accuracy is the key to successful piecing.

Pressing

In general, press seams toward the darker fabric. Press lightly in an up-and-down motion. Avoid using a very hot iron or over-ironing, which can distort shapes and blocks. Be especially careful when pressing bias edges, as they stretch easily. Arrows are provided for pressing.

Borders

When border strips are cut on the crosswise grain, piece the strips together to achieve the needed lengths.

Butted Borders

In most cases the side borders are sewn on first. When you have finished the quilt top, measure it through the center vertically. This will be the length to cut the side borders. Place pins at the centers of all four sides of the quilt top, as well as in the center of each side border strip. Pin the side borders to the quilt top first, matching the center pins. Using a ¼" seam allowance, sew the borders to the quilt top, and press toward the border.

Measure horizontally across the center of the quilt top, including the side borders. This will be the length to cut the top and bottom borders. Repeat the pinning, sewing, and pressing process.

Backing

Plan on making the backing a minimum of 8" longer and wider than the quilt top. Piece, if necessary. Trim the selvages before you piece to the desired size.

Batting

The type of batting to use is a personal decision; consult your local quilt shop. Cut batting approximately 8" longer and wider than your quilt top. Note that your batting choice will affect how much quilting is necessary. Check the manufacturer's instructions to see how far apart the quilting lines can be.

Basting

Basting keeps the quilt "sandwich" layers from shifting while you are quilting.

If you plan to machine quilt, pin baste the quilt layers together with safety pins placed a minimum of 3"–4" apart. Begin basting in the center and move toward the edges, first in vertical, then horizontal, rows. Try not to pin directly on the intended quilting lines.

If you plan to hand quilt, baste the layers together with thread, using a long needle and light-colored thread. Knot one end of the thread. Using stitches approximately the length of the needle, begin in the center and move out toward the edges in vertical and horizontal rows approximately 4" apart. Add two diagonal rows of basting.

Binding

Trim excess batting and backing from the quilt, even with the edges of the quilt top.

Double-Fold Straight-Grain Binding

If you want a ¼″ binding, cut the binding strips 2″ wide, and piece the binding strips together with diagonal seams to make a continuous binding strip. Trim the seam allowance to ¼″. Press the seams open.

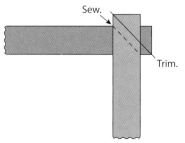

Sew from corner to corner.

Completed diagonal seam

Press the entire strip in half lengthwise, with wrong sides together. With raw edges even, start sewing the binding to the front edge of the quilt in the middle of one side of the quilt. Leave the first few inches of the binding unattached.

Stop ¼″ away from the first corner (see Step 1), and backstitch one stitch. Lift the presser foot and needle. Rotate the quilt a quarter-turn. Fold the binding at a right angle so it extends straight above the quilt and the fold forms a 45° angle in the corner (see Step 2). Then bring the binding strip down even with the edge of the quilt (see Step 3). Begin sewing at the folded edge. Repeat in the same manner at all corners.

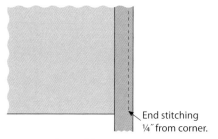

Step 1. Stitch to ¼″ from corner.

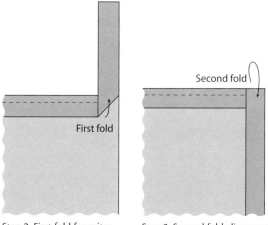

Step 2. First fold for miter   Step 3. Second fold alignment

Continue stitching until you are back near the beginning of the binding strip. See Finishing the Binding Ends for tips on finishing and hiding the raw edges of the ends of the binding.

Finishing the Binding Ends

Method 1:

After stitching around the quilt, fold under the beginning tail of the binding strip ¼″ so that the raw edge will be inside the binding after it is turned to the back of the quilt. Place the end tail of the binding strip over the beginning folded end. Continue to attach the binding, and stitch slightly beyond the starting stitches. Trim the excess binding. Fold the binding over the raw edges to the quilt back, and hand stitch, mitering the corners.

Method 2:

Fold the ending tail of the binding back on itself where it meets the beginning binding tail. From the fold, measure and mark the cut width of the binding strip. Cut the ending binding tail to this measurement. For example, if the binding is cut 2¼″ wide, measure 2¼″ from the fold on the ending tail of the binding, and cut the binding tail to this length.

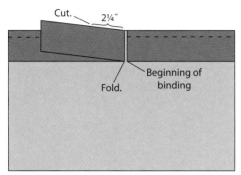

Cut binding tail.

Open both tails. Place one tail on top of the other tail at a right angle, with right sides together. Mark a diagonal line from corner to corner, and stitch on the line. Check that you've done it correctly and that the binding fits the quilt, and then trim the seam allowance to ¼″. Press open.

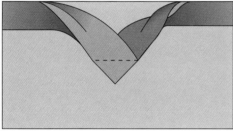

Stitch ends of binding diagonally.

Refold the binding and stitch this binding section in place on the quilt. Fold the binding over the raw edges to the quilt back, and hand stitch.

Note: For a short video on this technique, go to www. ctpub.com. Scroll down to the bottom of the page to *Consumer Resources* and click on *Quiltmaking Basics: Tips & Techniques for Quiltmaking and More.* Select *Completing a Binding with an Invisible Seam.*

About the Author

Monique Dillard, of Rockford, Illinois, was born in Winnipeg, Manitoba, Canada. Her love of quilting was nurtured by relatives in Canada who taught her the art of handwork and sewing. She parlayed her degree in mathematics into a genuine understanding of the need for accurate ¼″ seams, squared blocks, and precise cutting. She was a regular teacher at her local quilt shop for 15 years until her budding quilt design business, Open Gate, steered her career toward a national audience. These days, you can find Monique teaching across the United States at quilt guilds, weekend retreats, and quilt shops. Monique's classes always fill up fast with fans from previous classes and students eager to learn from this talented designer.

Follow Monique at www.opengatequilts.com as she continues to design unique and creative quilt patterns, books, and rulers.

Resources

The Fit to be Geese ruler, the Fit to be Square ruler, and the Fit to be Quarter ruler are available for wholesale and retail sales through www.opengatequilts.com.

the Quiltmaker's Club

More Patterns for Less

In this new series, we are gathering fabulous projects from established patternmakers into affordable books, all with the same high quality and accuracy you've come to expect from us. Now you get more patterns *and* more value!

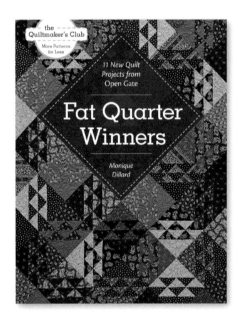

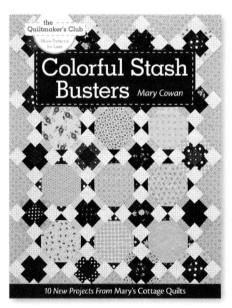

Available at your local retailer or **www.ctpub.com** *or* **800-284-1114 (USA)** ▪ **925-677-0377 (International)**

For a list of other fine books from C&T Publishing, visit our website to view our catalog online.

C&T PUBLISHING, INC.
P.O. Box 1456
Lafayette, CA 94549
800-284-1114

Email: ctinfo@ctpub.com
Website: www.ctpub.com

C&T Publishing's professional photography services are now available to the public. Visit us at www.ctmediaservices.com.

Tips and Techniques can be found at www.ctpub.com > Consumer Resources > Quiltmaking Basics: Tips & Techniques for Quiltmaking & More

For quilting supplies:

COTTON PATCH
1025 Brown Ave.
Lafayette, CA 94549
Store: 925-284-1177
Mail order: 925-283-7883

Email: CottonPa@aol.com
Website: www.quiltusa.com

Note: Fabrics shown may not be currently available, as fabric manufacturers keep most fabrics in print for only a short time.